T0355037

CHOOSE

LIFE TO THE FULLEST

90 DAYS TO THINKING
AND LIVING GREAT
PART 3

BECCA GUNYON, MCC

WESTBOW
PRESS®
A DIVISION OF THOMAS NELSON
& ZONDERVAN

WestBow Press books may be ordered through booksellers or by contacting:

WestBow Press
A Division of Thomas Nelson & Zondervan
1663 Liberty Drive
Bloomington, IN 47403
www.westbowpress.com
844-714-3454

ISBN: 978-1-6642-1254-1 (sc)
ISBN: 978-1-6642-1255-8 (e)

Print information available on the last page.

WestBow Press rev. date: 12/08/2020

Thank yous...

Thankful to my husband, Dan, who encourages me to write everyday.
Thankful for my son, Owin, who edits my books from a teen's perspective and encourages me to live my dreams.
Thankful for my daughter, Addi, who creates beauty, uses her creativity to help with all of the Instagram posts @chooselifetothefullest, and always speaks Jesus back to me.
Thankful to my son, Eben, who thanks me daily for being me.
Thankful to my son, John E, who flatters me with his funny compliments.
Thankful to my son, Anden, who asks me if I have "thought good thoughts" today.
Thankful to all the teenagers who previewed this book and gave their opinion.
Thankful to my family, Jim and Danise Owings, Josh and Meredith Owings, Matt and Abi Tuiasosopo, Micah Owings, JonMark Owings, and all my sweet nephews. What a blessing it is to be so close.
Thankful to Westbow Publishing for being so wonderful to work with.
Thankful to Lexie Fish for editing.
Thankful to Travis Fish for designing the cover.
Thankful to my Gwinnett Church Family and my Transit Team.

ENDORSEMENTS AFTER READING CHOOSE LIFE TO THE FULLEST BOOKS 1 AND 2...

"Becca and her husband Dan have been a vital part of our church for years now. They have sharpened us with their wisdom, care and love. Much of how they do this is by teaching us how to think. As Becca points out, the choice to live life to the fullest is exactly that—a choice. And it starts with our minds. I believe the next 90 days will shape and elevate your thoughts. When this happens, with the help of Jesus, our lives elevate as well."

Jeff Henderson, Author of Know What You're FOR

"Helping a teenager own their faith is hard. Finding a book that is easy to read, helpful, and practical may be harder. Becca Gunyon has created a resource that every student needs to read as they navigate their faith journey. So, if you are a parent or lead students, whether you're a student pastor or volunteer, you have got to get *Choose Life to the Fullest!*

Darren Swift, Associate Student's Director North Point Ministries

"There is nothing worth fighting for more than the faith of the next generation. After spending years in student ministry, I came to the conclusion that there has never been a more challenging time to grow up than now. Countless things compete daily for our attention and slowly cause us to drift from the things that matter most. I have known Becca and her family for decades and have always respected their commitment to the next generation. Paul told us that we can be transformed by the renewal of our minds. I believe this book helps us to see what it looks like to practically tap into the power that Paul was talking about. This is a great resource that will strengthen your entire family."

Grant Partrick, Passion City Church Cumberland Location Pastor

"Proverbs says, 'As a person thinks, so they are.' When Dr. Caroline Leaf says we have to "process over 50,000 thoughts each day and 80% are negative". How do we learn to combat negative thinking, our diminished value to society, and build self-worth? Choose Life provides a framework daily to reinforce thankfulness, plant seeds of hope, offer and allow positive to shed light on shadows of doubt, and provide an Anchor for the Soul. Providing this resource in a time when it's hard to combat the noise to define who we are, who to serve, what's our purpose, and rejoice in whatever circumstances we may be in, is so much needed. Like a tall, cool drink of cold water on a hot summer day. Thank you for faithfully sharing and encouraging us to think different and become different by Choosing Life to the Fullest."

Jim Owings, Founder of Lord's Way Ministries

"As we coach and care for the teenagers in our lives, not much is more important than encouraging them to practice renewing their minds. Becca's focus on spending a few moments each day to reflect on God's truth and focus on gratitude is a life changing practice not only for the young people who will build this habit, but also for the parents who are praying them through these tough years. I'm so excited for her to share these insights with a generation of kids who are hungry for them!"

Natalie Kitchen, North Point Leadership
Experience Residency Director

"Becca invites you to choose Life to the Fullest by waking up and thinking great thoughts again, and again. I could not recommend this book highly enough!"

Lexie Fish, Project Manager Gwinnett Church Transit

"As a parent, I believe it is life changing and something I will have to instill in my life and my children's lives. The concept of Living Life to the Fullest is a continuous process that we need to be reminded of often. As a teacher, I Love this book and the message it is trying to get across to students. Too many people do not know how to live or experience life to the fullest. It is a lifelong process and skill! Without God, we are nothing!"

Dr. Natalie Gibson, Teacher, Mother, Leader in student ministry

"Becca helped me learn to see myself through God's eyes and not others or my own. Her gentle kindness and servant spirit for God shine through her daily as she pours her life and heart into others more than herself. This book is God's heart through her pen expressing the aspiration she has for all people, that they journey to a daily relationship with God, learning to love themselves, the way that God loves them and in turn live their to the fullest.

Josh Owings, CEO of Owings Enterprises LLC,
GA. State Director US Elite Baseball

"God's heart for us all shines so beautifully through the words found in each devotional. Becca has humbly submitted her spirit, soul and body to declaring Gods truths in a simple, concise and easy to understand manner. The words cut through the chaos and distractions of life to refocus our minds, souls and spirits according to our true identity in Christ. Each devotional redirects our minds away from the lies of the enemy and this world back towards the truth which can only come from right believing and a personal relationship with Jesus. I'm blessed to be ministered to by such a courageous, faithful servant of God."

Zenda Griebenow, Director and Tennis Coach

ENDORSEMENTS FROM STUDENTS
(THEIR WORDS, THEIR AGE, AND SOMETHING THEY ENJOY)

"Choose Life to the Fullest has changed the way I think throughout the day. Every time I start to get down or think negative thoughts I remember to change them and focus on what's good. I have been 100% happier and I enjoy life more after reading and applying this book."

-*Owin, 17, Baseball*

"I believe that our thoughts effect the way we live our life. Sometimes it is difficult to change our negative thoughts and think positive. Choose Life to the Fullest is very encouraging and includes amazing advice for changing your thoughts."

-*Addi, 16, Basketball*

"Having struggled through difficult feelings such as heartbreak, depression, and anxiety myself, this book reminded me that God has given us the ability to *choose* an abundant life, despite the hardships we face. I was reminded that feelings are not always truth, and feelings do *not* control us! Through reading this, I was encouraged to stand up to lies in practical ways."

-Madison, College Student

"These daily devotions have impacted me emotionally and mentally. Whenever I feel like nothing can go my way. I think of the phrases and topics of the devotions and God always helps me power through it. All it takes is 5 minutes every day and I feel like a stronger person after."

-Derek 16, Baseball

"The 5 questions are the beginning of the devos help me to focus. Sometimes when I read the Bible, my mind will wander, but this not the case with Choose Life to the Fullest. It helps me to actively align myself with what God will teach me that day. I face a lot at school and this may be the only positive word I receive all day."

-JP, 16, Baseball and Crossfit

"I like them because they are short, powerful, and straight to the point. I get distracted and sleepy if people go on and on."

-Tolar, 13, Crossfit and Cross Country

"This devotional book is really making me think about Choosing Joy."

-August, 11, Reading Harry Potter

"I never thought about a lot of these questions."

-Pierce, 10, Baseball

"This is a fantastic devotional. I love the interaction for the daily question (What are 3 or 5 things?) It really made me think.

It really helped me focus on casting aside fears and focusing on God?"

-Emily, 13, Riding horses

"This devotional starts my day off with positivity and the right attitude. It reminds me daily of God's love for me and the people He has blessed me with."

-Ivan, 16, Basketball

"Choose Life to the Fullest provides truthful and encouraging reminders that start my day off with positivity and help me to focus on what is good. This devotional reminds me constantly of God's love for me and the many blessings that He has placed in my life."

-Claire, 16, Volleyball and Basketball

"Mom, I woke up this morning and started thinking of 5 things I was thankful for."

-Eben, 14, Tennis

"Life to the fullest has not just made an impact on the way I view myself, it has made a pivotal turn in my relationships with others. We can often start our day off on the wrong foot, but these daily devotionals have made a positive start to every day."

-Savannah, 18, Spending time outdoors

"This devotion really helped me see the many blessings I have been given throughout my life. It really helped me to see life in a more positive aspect. I would highly recommend this to anyone wanting a positive outlook on life."

-Julia, 17

"The 5 questions at the beginning of the lesson each day is what impacts me most, because it puts my focus on God and helps my day go better."

-*Christopher, 14, Basketball*

Thoughts from students who going through this book with their church small group:

"What I love most about the Devotional book is it helps me through my day and gives me a different perspective."

- *Eliza/ age 12/ softball*

"I wanted to say that the book taught me that God loves me and looks at me like I'm His treasure. The book taught me to love me for who I am because in His eyes I'm perfect! thank you!!"

-*Annabel/ age 12/ gymnast*

"The book Mrs. Becca wrote inspired me to know that I am not alone and God has given us so much that I could never be able to make up for -how kind He is. It helped me develop a better relationship because it gives you tasks that made me think about what I was doing wrong or what I was doing right. Now I feel stronger and my comfortable around Him and have done things that spread the word! Jesus took our mistakes, failures, and weakness and forgave them."

-*Lizzy/ age 12/loves to longboard*

"I love this devotional. it is a great way to get close to God and to practice gratitude."

-*Georgia/ age 13*

INTRODUCTION...

Oftentimes we seem to want to live life through the lens of someone else's life. We want to be popular, noticed, more athletic or attractive, more skilled, smarter or just...better. Instead, we end up seeing ourselves through false lenses. We see ourselves as ugly, ordinary, uncool, unwanted, awkward, dumb, or just not good enough.

We see other's lenses as better than ours and we try to change who we are, or we beat ourselves up. This leads us into spending our lives worrying about how we need to live life through someone else's lens. Because of this, we end up never enjoying the REAL us. The us that God created us to be. We're so busy looking at and worrying about our own outward appearance and how we are viewed by others that we never realize the amazing human God specially and uniquely crafted us into. It's like at the beach, you see the beautiful waves crash upon the sand and the water glistening in the sun, but when it's really bright you put on sunglasses. You still see the same view, it's just tinted. Looking through the sunglasses you don't see the unfiltered beauty of the beach, you see a less clear version.

This is also true in our own lives. When we put on our "sunglasses" (look through the lens of someone else) we only see a tinted version and not the REAL version of our lives. God made all of us different for a reason and he wants us to see ourselves for who we are, not for who we are not. Living our lives through a tinted version will only make us less happy and make our lives less enjoyable. Through God's lens he sees ALL of us as HIS perfect children and HIS most precious creation. If we can start to see ourselves through God's lens, we will become happier and live a more free and enjoyable life. - Written by Addi (high school student)

My daughter, Addi, wrote this introduction. It's my hope that by reading this book you will see yourself through God's lens. He is for you and wants you to live your life to the fullest!

What gifts has God given me?

1.
2.
3.
4.
5.

"God can pour on the blessings in astonishing ways so that you're ready for anything and everything..." (2 Corinthians 9:8 MSG)

"My focus creates my feelings." (Tommy Newberry)

We can focus on our gifts and blessings. When we look around, there is so much to be thankful for. However, sometimes to get to a place of thankfulness, we have to acknowledge our disappointments too.

What are my disappointments?

Once we expose it, we can give it to God, which takes away its power.

"God, I wanted _____, and this didn't go the way I thought, which makes me feel _____ (angry, disappointed, anxious). Please take all the negative away and lead me to focus on the good: Your gifts and Who You are. In Jesus name"

After a prayer of surrender we are free to focus on the GIFTS, the GOOD, and the BLESSINGS around us. When He frees our heart and mind from disappointments, we can live enjoying all of the good around us.

God, thank You for being the God who takes away pain and brings gifts. In Jesus name

What do I enjoy?

1.
2.
3.
4.
5.

"He replied, "Come along and see for yourself." (John 1:39 MSG)

There is a daily open invitation that Jesus invites us to. To see what He is up to we get to accept His invitation repeatedly. By whispering a simple prayer giving up our way (our control, our desires, our fears, our hopes), we accept His invitation to go on an adventure with him. His adventure is always better than what we might plan on our own.

Will I *"come along and see"* by letting go?

God, I accept Your invitation to adventure. I want what You want more than my will, I choose to trust Your heart for me. In Jesus name

DAY 3

What are five good things in my life?

1.
2.
3.
4.
5.

"Let Him love you." (Max Lucado)

God has relentless love for you, and he wants to know you. Most of us have a list of why we are unlovable. "If He really knew… (fill in the blank)." Yet God's response to our list would be, "Yes, I already knew about it. I know everything, and I still love You."

His love is not determined by our actions, thoughts or choices. His never-ending, all-consuming, tender, passionate, unconditional LOVE is based in who He is. His essence is love, so to Him we are all lovable. We get to choose to accept this truth, which is the foundation of living life to the fullest. Whether we choose His love or not, it never changes on His end. His love is always there. "Let Him love you." This is the best gift of all. His GREAT love covers our list of reasons why we feel unlovable and loves and accepts us there in that place.

Do I let God love me?

Are the messages I tell myself wrapped in His love?

When we let God's love permeate our life and become our foundation, everything changes.

God, fill my heart and mind with Your love. Forgive me for the things that hold me back from accepting Your love. I choose to let You love me. In Jesus name

DAY 4

Favorite GIFTS in my life:

1.
2.
3.
4.
5.

"Letting go of both the wrong and the resentment." (Matthew 6:12 AMP)

This phrase is part of the example prayer Jesus gives His disciples—His inner circle—to teach them how to talk to God. But, what does it mean? Resentment is that bad feeling we get when we can't forgive someone. Though it can feel justified, resentment swirls in our head and builds up our hearts, changing our countenance. It steals our joy and festers like a wound left unattended to.

Jesus teaches us to pray saying, *"Forgive us our debts, as we also have forgiven (left, remitted, let go of all debts and have given up resentment against) our debtors." (Mathew 6:12 AMPC)*

The word "debt" can also mean a sin. In this context, we can think of this as something someone does to us that is wrong. When we forgive others, we are giving them a gift. The word "given" is used here. In prayer, we can give God the resentment we feel toward others. I don't think this prayer had anything to do with feelings though. Forgiveness is a choice. We can pray, giving it God, which in turn blesses our health, heart, thoughts, feelings, and relationships.

Is there anyone in my life who I need to forgive?

God, I give You the resentment I feel for _____. I CHOOSE to let it go, even though I still feel _____. Heal my heart and the heart of the person who wronged me. In Jesus name

I like this about me:

1.
2.
3.
4.
5.

"And we know in ALL things God works for the good of those who love Him, who have been called according to His purpose." (Romans 8:28 NIV)

When I ask the question above, it's very hard for people to answer. Most of us can quickly say five things we *don't* like about ourselves. But five things we *do* like—on the inside or the outside—this takes some thought. When we only focus on our flaws, we feel defeated and it doesn't help us grow. However, when we focus on our gifts, strengths, and areas of growth, we feel motivated. We get to choose to work on our weaknesses and focus on our strengths.

With the gifts God has given me, who can I help and give life to today?

God, I invite You in. Help me to see me the way You do. Work in me and through me. In Jesus name

DAY 6

Who gives life to me?

1.
2.
3.
4.
5.

Living out thankfulness for the people around us keeps our focus on the good.

"For God so loved the world that He gave His one and only Son." (John 3:16 NIV)

For God SO loved each of us. I can better embrace the magnitude of God's love for me when I am very aware of my humanness. God is there with us at every second so He sees every moment, hears every word and knows every thought. Nothing is hidden. He knows the real and the messy and, there in that place, He loves us. This amazes me! People enjoy and love us at our best and in our health. God loves us here too. However, His love goes beyond the good to the very core of our struggle and loves us enough to pick us up, wrap us in His love, heal our wounds, and make beauty out of our story.

What do you need God's love to heal today?

God, I love that You love me where I am at, not where I think I should be. I invite You into the broken places. In Jesus name

DAY 7

I am thankful for:

1.
2.
3.
4.
5.

"Jesus answered, 'If you knew the generosity of God and who I am, you would be asking me for a drink, and I would give you fresh, living water.'" (John 4:10 MSG)

"If you knew the generosity of God and who I am." Life lived to the fullest is centered in being aware of God's generous heart and Who Jesus is. Jesus brings us the healing heart of God. Sometimes we resist, we have our reason why His love seems incomplete, or why we aren't enough. His love covers all of these by saying, *"If you knew who I am."*

No matter how long we have been in a relationship with Jesus, we must daily remember Who He is and what that means for us. The love of God shown in the life of Jesus is enough to fill every void in our life. His love is enough to battle all of our insecurity, worry, and frustrations. If we lived wrapped in the truths of Jesus, our heart will be full and our mind will choose to think great! Remembering Him leads to a full life!

Do I live aware of God's love for me?

God, thank You for _____. Remind me of the power and love of Jesus throughout each day. May I embrace Your heart for me. In Jesus name

DAY 8

What is good in my life?

1.
2.
3.
4.
5.

Sometimes I get stuck in these questions, especially if it's raining, dreary, and cold. It takes more effort to think of the amazing. These are a few of my answers:

Friends, people who know me and love me anyway.

My siblings and brother and sister in-law who I can call at any time and they will help me.

Music, singing a song can change a boring day into one of laughter.

When we get stuck thinking about the good, what we are thankful for, and God's gifts to us, our face shows it. Whether we realize it or not, we wear our thoughts. Even when we put on a mask and fake a smile, what we are thinking peaks through. When we think God thoughts, we reflect His love.

Reading about Jesus in the book of John, I like to picture His face. My guess is that he looked peaceful, strong, and loving, that he had a countenance both inviting and warm. His face must have been so unthreatening, because He always drew a crowd. I want to be like that, don't you? Being a person who makes people feel like life is better because they are with us, that would reflect Jesus.

We get the GIFT of reflecting Him.

"Nothing between us and God, our faces shining with the brightness of His face. And so we are transfigured much like the Messiah, our lives gradually becoming brighter and more beautiful as God enters our lives and we become like him." (3 Corinthians 3:19 MSG)

Do I think about things that are life-giving to myself and others?

Do I want to wear the thoughts I think on my face?

God, I want my face to shine *"with the brightness of"* Your face. I want to be a reflection of Your heart. I give You all of the life stuff that competes for my joy, peace, and love. In Jesus name

DAY 9

What is good in my life?

1.
2.
3.
4.
5.

"Therefore, as we have opportunity, let us do good to all people, especially to those who belong to the family of believers." (Galatians 6:10 NIV)

It's fun to look for ways to "do good," and we can do this every day. Looking for ways to do something good for others takes the focus off of ourselves. Our feelings of insecurity, inadequacy, and anxiety seem to go away when we quit giving them attention. We can starve these negative feelings that seek to drag us down by thinking, "Who can I bless or do something good for today?"

On days I am really struggling with my thoughts or feelings, I have found that encouraging others helps me to quit focusing on my "stuff." Doing good is one way to live life to the fullest.

Who can I "do good to" today?

God, here are my own thoughts about me and life. I want to get out of my stuff and do good to others. I invite You to lead me in this. In Jesus name

DAY 10

What am I thankful for?

1.
2.
3.
4.
5.

"But when he, the Spirit of truth, comes, he will guide you into all the truth. He will not speak on his own; he will speak only what he hears, and he will tell you what is yet to come. He will glorify me because it's from me that he will receive what he will make known to you. All that belongs to the Father is mine. That is why I said the Spirit will receive from me what he will make known to you." (John 16:13-14 NIV)

It's really hard to explain His Spirit or to make it relatable. The Spirit of God becomes more real when we invite Jesus in. Inviting Jesus in means saying, "I want You to be part of my life." When we do this, God's Spirit starts working on our heart and mind, and in our feelings and struggles. Maybe we wish He would speak louder or work faster, but I like to think of His Spirit as the wind all around me—constantly moving and working. Or the air, something I rely on moment by moment to sustain life. The Spirit of God is the essence of God He left here with us to help guide our steps.

Can I invite Jesus to be part of my life? Why or why not?

Jesus, I want You to be part of my life. I give You me. In Your name

Good things in my life: (For me it's hot chocolate on a cold day.)

1.
2.
3.
4.
5.

"Now He (Jesus) is the exact likeness of the unseen God (the visible representation of the invisible): He is the Firstborn of all creation." *(Colossians 1:15)*

The stories of Jesus reveal the heart of God. If I ever feel distant from God, reading a story from when Jesus walked here reminds me of God's character. Jesus spoke truth wrapped in love. He gave grace to the undeserving. He loved the children and the seemingly ordinary. He was so dynamic a crowd followed Him. Yet even though He was perfect, He often found a quiet place to pray and talk to God.

Looking at Jesus explains the heart of God. In a world of unknowns, God's heart is a safe place to entrust our lives to.

What do I think about God?

What do I think God sees when He thinks about me?

God, remind me Who You are through the life of Jesus and help
me to choose to see You as a God who I can entrust my life to.
In Jesus name

DAY 12

I am thankful to God for:

1.
2.
3.
4.
5.

"But the Holy Spirit produces this kind of fruit in our lives: love, joy, peace, patience, kindness, goodness, faithfulness, gentleness, and self-control." (Galatians 5:22 NLT)

When you remember a message or talk from four or five years, that is an impact! Years ago at Gwinnett Church the New Year's Message was about choosing a Fruit of the Spirit to embrace for a year. As soon as we got in the car, all seven of us (me, my husband, and our five kids) started talking about which fruit we would choose. My kids chose for me saying, "Mom, you are joyful and loving, but you are NOT peaceful," they all agreed! Grabbing a slice of humble pie, I admitted they were right.

Their honesty that day created a desire in me to change and grow, so for years I have been diving into peace. Tomorrow I will share what this looked like for me. I am so thankful to have been given honest feedback. For four years peace has been my fruit to embrace for the year. I'll keep choosing peace until it becomes second nature. Then I'll begin again with another fruit.

What fruit do you choose?

God, please give me Your fruits of the Spirit. Show me what needs to change in my thinking so I can embrace the fruit You have for me. In Jesus name

If you've tracked along since Book 1, you've heard this story before. Choosing peace is a constant choice, and sometimes a battle. If you have something you are struggling with, like I did with having peace, you need to face it every day.

DAY 13

What gives me joy?

1.
2.
3.
4.
5.

In order to fully embrace the Fruit of the Spirit, peace, I had to take an honest look in the mirror and figure out the root of why I was not peaceful...and I found that I didn't trust God completely. I had given Him my life in pre-school, but I still held on to my worries, doubts and fears and somehow thought it would help. My constant worry was hard to face. I had to embrace the reality that God is in control and I am not. I can pray and I can follow His path, but the result is up to Him, not me. Whew, this took the pressure off! Anytime I'm stressed I have to remember this and relinquish my desire to control.

Next, I had to find ways to repeatedly change my thinking. Finding a verse to repeatedly tell myself helped. Like, *"For we are God's masterpiece." (Ephesians 2:10 NLT)*

God and I talk about peace a lot. He reminds me to "rest and trust." I hear this echo in my head nonstop.

After years of letting peace be my choice of fruits, which has meant battling my worry, anxiety, and what ifs, I have made progress toward peacefulness. But I am not sure that I would call myself peaceful yet, so I think I will choose peace for another year.

Is there anything that keeps you from living out the fruit (quality) you chose?

God, I invite You into my journey toward _____ (love, joy, peace, patience, kindness, goodness, gentleness, faithfulness, or self-control). Give me a strategy for growing in this area. In Jesus name

Where can I see God working in my life?

1.

2.

3.

4.

5.

"Come and see." (John 1:39 NLT)

The life of Jesus shows us the heart of God. When I need a refresh, I go back to the Gospels of Matthew, Mark, Luke, and John. These stories share the center of Christianity. Jesus began his ministry inviting his disciples into a relationship. He invited them to come and check out what God had in store for them and He does the same for us!

He tells us to *"Come and see"* what a relationship with Him is like. Come and see what happens when we pray. Come and see how He speaks to us when we read our Bible. Come and see life become enjoyable when we choose to accept His love. Come and see what changes in us when we give Him our life, our heart, our mind, our thoughts, our hurt, our dreams, our hopes, our relationships, our moments.

Will I accept His invitation?

Jesus, I accept Your invitation, as I choose to follow You, show me Your heart.

DAY 15

What I am thankful for:

1.
2.
3.
4.
5.

"Celebrate God all day, every day." (Philippians 4:4 MSG)

"The mind cannot at the same time be full of God and full of fear." (Be Anxious for Nothing, Max Lucado) In this book, Max explains one antidote for anxiety is celebrating God. Even in moments when we don't feel like celebrating, feelings don't have to control us unless we let them.

What can I celebrate about God?

Thinking about the good and the things worth celebrating takes the focus off of me, my situation, my unknowns and anxieties. One way to do this is taking a look at Jesus and His life when He lived here. The book of John in the bible is a great place to start. I think Jesus was strong, tender, powerful and loving, but I also think He was funny. This can be seen by the way He handles a few situations in the Bible. I encourage you to look and read about the life of Jesus. Everyone wanted to be with Him, and many stories are recorded where He went fishing with his friends. These twelve friends left everything to hang out with and follow Jesus. Something about Jesus drew crowds, He was not boring or aloof. Who Jesus is changes lives! To celebrate God, we have to know Who He is and this is life-changing.

God, show me more of You through the life of Jesus. In Jesus name

What kind things do I tell myself?

1.
2.
3.
4.
5.

"Be kind to one another, tenderhearted, forgiving one another, as God in Christ forgave you." (Ephesians 4:32 ESV)

I remember what an epiphany it was for me when I realized God wanted me to be kinder to myself. At first it just felt weird. It was much easier to be negative and demanding than to be kind to myself in my thoughts. Somewhere along the way, I realized I could not give people the kindness of Jesus wholeheartedly unless I embraced it for myself.

This is not a one time realization, but daily asking myself if what I think about myself is based on the love and acceptance of Jesus.

One night when I picked up my kids from tennis lessons, I heard their tennis coach say, "When you go home write down three things you did great tonight." This thought stayed with me the whole way home. What if you and I finished our day by thinking:

What are three ways I improved today?

Who is someone I helped?

What did I do better today than yesterday?

Am I listening to my voice about me or God's voice about me?

Feelings about ourselves change when we see ourselves through the eyes of Jesus. He has so much love and grace to pour into us and this motivates us towards greatness. Every other motivator runs out at some point.

What am I telling myself at the end of the day?

Throughout the day?

Would God tell me this? If not, what do I think he *is* saying?

He constantly whispers words of love to us because His very essence is love! To Him, we are all fully loved!

God, pour love into my heart, may I see me through Your eyes. Remind me what You say about me. In Jesus name

What do I like about myself?

1.
2.
3.
4.
5.

"Jesus took one look up and said, 'You're John's son, Simon? From now on your name is Cephas' (or Peter, which means Rock)." (John 1:42 MSG)

Jesus took one look at Peter and saw something in him. In that moment, Jesus changed Peter's name and spoke over him what he would become. Can you imagine what that would be like?

We call ourselves all kinds of names in our mind, or even out loud. Many of these names don't make us feel great about ourselves.

There are also names God calls us, titles that empower us to become who God is growing us to be. "Treasure, Masterpiece,

Chosen, Child of God, Mine," just a few of the names God calls us.

What names do I call myself?

We can choose to think about what God calls us instead of the names we or others call ourselves in negativity. His names change the way we see ourselves.

God, remind me when I am calling myself something negative that You call me, "loved, treasured, masterpiece, child of God." In Jesus name

I am thankful for:

1.
2.
3.
4.
5.

"She went ahead anyway, telling the servants, 'Whatever he (Jesus) tells you, do it.'" (John 2:5 MSG)

Jesus' first miracle recorded was at a party. This in itself tells me so much about the heart of God and how he feels about celebrating. Reading about this miracle always makes me stop and think. Jesus' mom pushed Him to do this miracle. She must have known Jesus was capable of doing something miraculous. She must have known His heart. She must have known He would provide for this celebration. I love her advice, *"Whatever He tells you, do it!"*

Thinking about that advice in our own lives, what is God telling us to do? There are so many life-giving instructions in the Bible:

trust, forgive, rest, love, persevere. Her instructions have been echoing in my head, *"Whatever He tells you, do it!"*

What is God leading you to do?

Does anything hold you back from this?

God, help me to trust Your heart for me, so that I will follow what You are leading me to do. In Jesus name

DAY 19

Good things in my life:

1.
2.
3.
4.
5.

"During the time he was in Jerusalem, those days of the Passover Feast, many people noticed the signs he was displaying and, seeing they pointed straight to God, entrusted their lives to him." (John 2:23-25 MSG)

Looking to Him instead of our circumstances or those around us leads us to trust in the Heart of God, displayed through the life of Jesus. Seeing His heart and His actions and hearing His words led people to entrust their lives to Him.

Entrusting our life to Him leads to peace. Although we long for control, the pressure of thinking we are in control of our world can lead to anxiety or restlessness. An unexplainable peace fills our minds and hearts when we open-handedly say, "God, I trust You with me—my life, my thoughts, my dreams, my family, my school or work, my future, what people think about me." I find myself saying this daily, giving my stuff to Him, it immediately takes the pressure off of me.

Does anything hold me back from entrusting my "stuff" to God?

God, I trust You with me: my life, my thoughts, my dreams, my family, my school or work, my future, what people think about me. As I give you these things, please fill my heart, mind and emotions with Your peace. In Jesus name

DAY 20

What do I love?

1.

2.

3.

4.

5.

"This is how much God loved the world: He gave his Son, his one and only Son. And this is why: so that no one need be destroyed; by believing in him, anyone can have a whole and lasting life. God didn't go to all the trouble of sending his Son merely to point an accusing finger, telling the world how bad it was. He came to help, to put the world right again." (John 3:16-17 MSG)

The love of God is both simple and complex. The simplicity is that we can choose to accept, believe, and embrace Jesus and give our lives to Him. The complexity is remembering God's love every moment. When life gets tough, we can forget that the same God who made the oceans and the skies, and everything in between, takes care of us too. We can forget that, in the end, everything is going to be perfect. We can forget that His love is big enough to cover all of our insecurity, pain, disappointment and more.

"For God so loved the world." That is you and me. He "so loved" us! Even when His love does not feel like enough to fill our heart, it is! Living life to the fullest is about embracing His love and choosing to shape our minds and lives around it.

How can I embrace God's love for me?

God, when my thoughts go negative (about life, others, or myself) remind me that Your love is SO big. Help me to focus on the good things around me. In Jesus name

DAY 21

What makes me smile?

1.
2.
3.
4.
5.

Everyday, we get the choice to focus on the things that make us smile, or the things that make us sigh with dread.

"The One (Jesus) that God sent speaks God's words. And don't think he rations out the Spirit in bits and pieces. The Father loves the Son extravagantly. He turned everything over to him so he could give it away—a lavish distribution of gifts. That is why whoever accepts and trusts the Son gets in on everything, life complete and forever! And that is also why the person who avoids and distrusts the Son is in the dark and doesn't see life. All he experiences of God is darkness, and an angry darkness at that." (John 3:36-38 MSG)

If you read everyday, you probably noticed each verse from the last week has been from the book of John. When I worked in

Young Life, they would remind us often to learn more about the life of Jesus by re-reading the Gospels. This book of the bible is so life-giving!

This passage in John talks about the heart of God. Jesus gets to give away God's heart and bless us with "a lavish distribution of gifts." Wow! This amazes me! Real life is found in living in the heart of God, accepting and thinking about His gifts, and inviting Jesus in.

What gifts has God blessed me with recently?

God, thank You that You are the Giver of great gifts. Help me to focus on the gifts from You. Jesus, I invite You into every aspect of my life.

What makes me laugh?

1.
2.
3.
4.
5.

"Many of the Samaritans from that village committed themselves to him because of the woman's witness: 'He knew all about the things I did. He knows me inside and out!' They asked him to stay on, so Jesus stayed two days. A lot more people entrusted their lives to him when they heard what he had to say. They said to the woman, 'We're no longer taking this on your say-so. We've heard it for ourselves and know it for sure. He's the Savior of the world!'" (John 4:39-42 MSG)

In this story, many believed because of the woman's testimony. This story is amazing! A woman—who made many wrong choices in her life—met Jesus, went back home, and brought her town to Him. Something about the love of Jesus must have been so transforming that the change was visible. Even though she knew Jesus knew all of her story, including the bad parts, she took comfort in the truth that, *"He knows me inside and out."*

As we invite Jesus into our lives daily, we can share Him with others. Our story is powerful!

How can I share my story with others?

God, thank You for knowing me completely and loving me completely. Help me to share my testimony and bring others to Your heart. In Jesus name

DAY 23

Whose life can I make better today?

1.
2.
3.

"The one who blesses others is abundantly blessed; those who help others are helped." (Proverbs 11:25 MSG)

When we give life to others, we get outside of ourselves. We see what others are walking through. By giving an encouraging word, text, or message, we can change someone's day. If our thoughts about ourselves start going in a negative direction, one of the best things to do is to go find someone to encourage, give to, or help. As we give to others we can invite God into the process. He multiplies our gift and makes it even bigger!

Who can I give life to today?

God, show me who needs a word encouragement or act of kindness today, In Jesus name

DAY 24

What do I enjoy?

1.
2.
3.
4.
5.

"There was a certain official from the king's court whose son was sick. When he heard that Jesus had come from Judea to Galilee, he went and asked that he come down and heal his son, who was on the brink of death...Jesus simply replied, 'Go home. Your son lives.' The man believed the bare word Jesus spoke and headed home. On his way back, his servants intercepted him and announced, 'Your son lives!' He asked them what time he began to get better. They said, 'The fever broke yesterday afternoon at one o'clock.' The father knew that that was the very moment Jesus had said, 'Your son lives.' That clinched it. Not only did he but his entire household believed." (John 4:46-48, 50-54 MSG)

In the Bible, the miraculous power of Jesus changed lives and homes. He still does this today. He reminds me to pray daily, instead of living in the swirl of thoughts. Ask BIG. Ask for miracles. Ask for favor. Ask for healing. Ask for His heart to transform lives. The man in the story asked for healing for his son. Jesus healed him and, because of this, his entire household believed (which back then, an entire household was a lot of people). So let's ask BIG.

What can I ask God for today?

God, You know my heart, please _____. In Jesus name

God, Thank You For:

1.
2.
3.
4.
5.

"A huge wind blew up, churning the sea. They were maybe three or four miles out when they saw Jesus walking on the sea, quite near the boat. They were scared senseless, but he reassured them, 'It's me. It's all right. Don't be afraid.' So they took him on board. In no time they reached land—the exact spot they were headed to." (John 6:16-21 MSG)

This miracle of Jesus scared His friends. Even though they were walking and living with Him, they didn't expect Him to do the miraculous. We hope for amazing things in our life. Maybe we want to see Jesus do something extraordinary, but, just like his disciples, we are scared sometimes.

This story led me to ask myself, "Do I expect Jesus to do something miraculous? If not, what holds me back? Why am I so surprised if He does?" You can ask yourself these same questions.

Jesus, thank You that You are the God of miracles. Please make miracles in this situation _____ I choose to trust that You can. In Jesus name.

DAY 26

What makes me smile?

1.
2.
3.
4.
5.

"When Jesus looked up and saw a great crowd coming toward him, he said to Philip, 'Where shall we buy bread for these people to eat?' He asked this only to test him, for he already had in mind what he was going to do." (John 6:5-6 NIV)

The heart of Jesus is threaded throughout this story. I love that Jesus asked Philip where they could buy bread for all of these people. Did He ask with a smile on his face because He already knew?

I wonder if He does that with us. He asks us, "How are we going to do this?" He's looking for us to choose faith in Him.

This morning God woke me up and whispered, "Rest and Trust." He does this often. His whisper led to writing a list of all of the things I need to trust God with and choosing to let go of the swirl in my brain and trust His heart, that He already knows what He is going to do.

What is the swirl in your mind?

What do you need to trust Him with?

Within two minutes I wrote down 10 things I know He can do. *"All we do is trust Him enough to let Him do it." (Ephesians 2:7 MSG).* We don't have to "feel" like trusting, we can choose it (again and again). His heart for us is good. He already knows what He is going to do, so we can trust and rest.

God, I give You the swirl in my brain. I choose to trust You with the things I worry about. Please give me Your rest and peace so I can live life to the full. In Jesus name

This is good in my life:

1.

2.

3.

4.

5.

"Every person the Father gives me eventually comes running to me. And once a person is with me, I hold on and don't let go." (John 6:37 MSG)

We get to choose what we think in each moment. What we are thinking affects our attitude, which affects the way people respond to us. Some moments are easy to choose joy, others take more effort. Living life around people, we get to choose how we respond to them and think about others each moment. We get to see others through the lens of Jesus. He promises to walk through life with us. Taking an honest look at our thoughts is so powerful.

What do I think about most of the time?

Is it life-giving?

Jesus, I invite You into my moments. May I see myself and others through Your eyes, and when I do this may my thoughts be life-giving! In Your name

DAY 28

What makes me smile?

1.
2.
3.
4.
5.

"Therefore if any person is (ingrafted) in Christ (the Messiah) he is a new creation altogether; the old (previous moral and spiritual condition) has passed away. Behold, the fresh and new has come!" (2 Corinthians 5:17 AMPC)

I love that we get a new start everyday! We get to choose better than we did yesterday. We can let go of the mistakes or pain from the days before. If we drag yesterday into today we can feel tired, burdened, and, sometimes, even guilty. God gave us the gift of Jesus, which means new life everyday!

Do I dwell on thoughts of yesterday? How?

What does a fresh new start look like for me?

God, please take away any negativity or guilt that I feel from yesterday, help me to embrace Your forgiveness. I want to live in the realization that I am "ingrafted" in Christ Jesus. In His name

What am I looking forward to?

1.
2.
3.
4.
5.

"Jesus straightened up and asked her, 'Woman, where are they? Has no one condemned you?' 'No one, sir,' she said. 'Then neither do I condemn you,' Jesus declared. 'Go now and leave your life of sin.'" (John 8:10-11)

The world and our own thoughts can shame us. Living under a cloud of shame is not motivating. Jesus offers freedom from guilt and shame. The unconditional, never-ending love of Jesus releases us. We can embrace His forgiveness, which frees us to change our behavior.

Do I embrace His forgiveness?

God, thank You for Your heart for me. I accept the love and forgiveness of Jesus, please forgive me and free me from my sin. In Jesus name

DAY 30

What do I like about my life?

1.

2.

3.

4.

5.

"We take captive every thought to make it obedient to Christ." (2 Corinthians 10:5 NIV)

Most of us have an inner phrase that drives us. I realized this after reading one of John Eldredge's books. This phrase is not God's voice, but one I created in my own head. When I identified mine, I realized how it played out in everything I did or said, stealing my joy. My phrase was, "it's not enough." In whatever I was doing, (writing, counseling, serving, working) and in every relationship (as a wife, mom, sister, friend) I heard this phrase repeating in my head.

When I get sad or overwhelmed, I can tell that I am listening to this inner phrase and not God's voice. His voice motivates us to live wrapped in His love and out of that to give His love to others.

What negative thing do you tell yourself?

Is this helping you?

Do you want to change this phrase?

Once you identify the negative sentence you are telling yourself, you can change it to something positive that God says about you.

What is the opposite of the negative sentence I tell myself?

For me, whenever I start to think that what I'm doing isn't good enough, I stop and say to myself, "Because of Jesus, I *am* enough."

Jesus, I invite You into my thoughts. Remind me You want me to be motivated by what Your love says about me.

DAY 31

What do I like about myself?

1.
2.
3.
4.
5.

Most of us can quickly come up with five dislikes about ourselves. However, it's life-giving to ask ourselves what gifts God has given you that you enjoy about yourself.

"The Spirit can make life. Sheer muscle and willpower don't make anything happen." (John 6:63 MSG)

For those of us that like to work hard, this verse can stop us in our tracks. We can work and strive, but without inviting God into the process most of us find out at some point this isn't real and full life. Everything feels meaningless without God's hand in it. *"Everything is meaningless." (Ecclesiastes 1:2 MSG)*

In contrast, when we invite Jesus into our daily tasks, relationships, dreams, and decisions, this is when real life happens. Our thoughts about life change because when God is part of things life feels fulfilling. We have a purpose. We take the pressure off ourselves. Prayer becomes our response.

Am frustrated trying to do life with my own strength?

How can I rely more on God?

God, I need You. Sometimes I forget that I need You and try to do things on my own. I know You are always with me, I just forget to invite You into my stress, pressure, and responsibilities. I need Your Spirit constantly at work in my mind, heart, emotions, conversations, and actions. I invite the power of Jesus into every aspect of my life.

DAY 32

What is good in my life?

1.

2.

3.

4.

5.

"Jesus went across to the Mount of Olives, but He was soon back in the Temple again. Swarms of people came to him. He sat down and taught them." (John 8:1 MSG)

"Swarms" of people came to find Jesus. What was it about Jesus that captured their attention? Was it His voice? Was it the way He looked at them? Was it the way He made them feel? I can imagine He exuded love in a way that quenched each heart. Sitting there listening to His truth must have been so peaceful and powerful that "swarms" of people came to Him.

Because God created us for a relationship with Him, we all long for closeness with Him. In the business of life, we long for Jesus. Coming to Jesus means listening to God, which can be by reading a Bible verse and spending time thinking about it. Coming to God is also about talking to Him—in our mind or out loud. We can give Him our worries, thank Him for the good in our life, and invite Him into our day (our decisions, our thoughts, our relationships, our work or school).

When Jesus walked here on earth, his love was so powerful, so incredible, that crowds followed wherever he went. This same love is available to us every moment!

God, fill my heart with the love of Jesus. May Your love heal any brokenness. May my heart be so full of Your love that it spills out on others around me. In Jesus name

DAY 33

What makes me smile?

1.
2.
3.
4.
5.

"Jesus once again addressed them: 'I am the world's Light. No one who follows me stumbles around in darkness. I provide plenty of light to live in.'" (John 8:12 MSG)

Have you ever been in a room where it's pitch black? When all the lights are out, we can't find our way. Being surrounded by darkness gives us a feeling of being lost. In a world of unknowns, we don't have to feel this way. Jesus promises to be our Light. Following Jesus is like turning the lights on in a dark room. Living in His light consists of a daily living in relationship with Him.

Moment by moment, we can find our way, living in His light, by thinking or whispering a prayer when we are stressed, focusing on a Bible verse when our mind goes to negative thoughts, reminding ourselves that our identity comes from Him. For He made us and loves us. We get to choose to live in His light.

Do I ever feel lost?

When and why?

God, remind me that I'm not lost, because Jesus provides light to live in. I invite Jesus to do life with me in every moment. Remind me throughout the day that I am not alone and You are always there guiding my path. Show me Your light. In Jesus name

What am I thankful for?

1.
2.
3.
4.
5.

So if the Son sets you free, you are free through and through." (John 8:36 MSG)

Struggle, worry, anxiety, depression, anger, addiction...all of these feel like bondage. Being trapped in a behavior or habit feels bigger than what we can handle on our own. Most of us want a quick solution to everything. However, living free from our struggle (whatever it may be) is attainable by living close to the heart of Jesus. Freedom can be a journey of little steps. One day we will wake up and realize we aren't struggling with that habit anymore.

When I was 16, I hit a wall. The eating disorder I used to deal with stress, perfectionism, and people pleasing was exposed. This struggle felt like chains and yet, it was comfortable. Steps to freedom were small and sometimes I failed. However, complete freedom came and now that 8-10 year struggle feels like a lifetime away. Living free is possible!

The secret to complete freedom came by retraining my brain. For a year, I told myself a quote about identity, "Define yourself radically as one beloved by God, God's love for you and choice of you define your worth. ACCEPT that and let it become the most important thing in your life" (Brennan Manning, Abba's Child). Every single time I started saying self-defeating things to myself or worrying, I would say this quote. Some days, I said it hundreds of times. Over time my thoughts about me changed, my emotions changed, and eventually my behavior changed. This may sound so simple...because it is! Freedom comes from repeatedly living in the truth of Jesus and who He says we are.

Do I live free?

If you are struggling with anything, I encourage you to find a quote or verse and let it become the truth you cling to. Say this phrase to yourself over and over again for months, let it change the way you see yourself.

God, I invite You into my thoughts about me. Set me free from what I struggle with. Remind me constantly of how much You love me, for this is my true identity. In Jesus name

What makes me laugh?

1.
2.
3.
4.
5.

"'Then how was your blindness cured?' they asked. 'The man called Jesus.'" (John 9:10-11 Philips)

Jesus opens our eyes to see real life. In this passage the man was blind and Jesus healed him. When asked how he was healed his explanation was simple, Jesus. In a world full of self-help solutions, programs, and slogans, going to Jesus can seem too simple. If we dive into Who the Bible says Jesus is and what He promises to do for us, we can see clearly that His love is healing, His heart is a safe place, and His name has power. Looking to Him takes the pressure off of us.

Is my vision of God and life clouded, or can I see clearly?

God, I want the healing love of Jesus to fill my life and my heart. I give all of me to You, please heal the broken places. Please forgive and restore me. In Jesus name

DAY 36

What am I looking forward to?

1.
2.
3.
4.
5.

At times, life can feel routine. Especially on rainy days when it's dreary outside, it's good to think about what we are looking forward to.

In John chapter 9, the story of Jesus healing a blind man is told. The religious rulers at the time didn't believe Jesus could perform this miracle, so they interrogated the man and his parents. Eventually, they threw him (the healed man) out on the street. Jesus finds the man and asks him if he believes in Him. Yet even after being healed by Jesus, he does not recognize His voice.

"Jesus said, 'You're looking at Him, Don't you recognize my voice?'" (John 9:37 MSG)

Do we recognize God at work in our life?

When He reminds us of a Bible verse or a song, that is one way He speaks to us! The heart of Jesus loves us and is always pursuing us.

God, show me the heart of Jesus and help me to know His voice. In Jesus name

DAY 37

What am I thankful for:

1.
2.
3.
4.
5.

"He calls his own sheep by name and leads them out...he leads them and they follow because they are familiar with his voice." (John 10:3-5 MSG)

In this passage, we are referred to as sheep being led by a shepherd. He calls us by name and we follow Him because we are familiar with His voice and have faith in where He is leading us. I totally relate with the sheep. I believe He is asking for simple trust and a heart of surrender.

With all of the noise around us it can feel complicated to follow His voice and direction. Trust is a choice. Daily, we can entrust our lives and situations to God by simply saying, "I give all of this (life stuff) to you, and I give You me." Walking with God is about continually giving up our lives to Him. Listening and following Him involves following the guidelines He gave us and being willing to go where He asks. Even when life feels hard or unfair, God has the best life for us!

Am I following God's way of life for me?

If so, how? If not, why?

God, I give You me. I trust Your heart for me. I believe Jesus died and rose for me. Please forgive my sin and the rebellion that keeps me from You. In Jesus name

DAY 38

I am thankful for:

1.
2.
3.
4.
5

"A thief is only there to steal and kill and destroy. I (Jesus) came so they can have real and eternal life, more and better life than they ever dreamed of." (John 10:10 MSG)

Jesus came for all of us, the broken, the lost, the doubting, the mourning, the hopeful, the joyful, the searching. He came to give us real life, *"A better life than we ever dreamed of."* When life is hard, we can wonder where He is or what He is up to. Yet if we choose His way and walk with Him, no matter what happens, we will be okay. Whatever we are going through can be turned into something that makes our life more full. God can work everything together for His glory.

Real life is centered in living moment by moment aware that God loves us with a tender, passionate, and unconditional love as seen in the life of Jesus.

Do I live aware of God's love?

God, I want real life. Fill my heart with Your love, drive away the thief. I choose the real full life You have for me. In Jesus name

What is good in my life?

1.
2.
3.
4.
5.

"The thief comes only to steal and kill and destroy; I (Jesus) have come that they may have life, and have it to the full." (John 10:10 NIV)

Did you see *Spiderman Far from Home*? Remember the plot twist at the end? The evil villain makes everyone think Spiderman is responsible for all the bad things that have happened.

I have this theory: the Thief (Satan, the devil, the enemy) tries to convince us to blame God when bad things happen. Why would he do this? Why do all villains do this?

If we blame God, we get angry with Him or we distance ourselves from Him. We resist the greatest thing of all, His love. This love knows no boundaries, it heals that place deep inside of us where we don't like ourselves. His love is enough to cover our weaknesses and failures and give us hope. His love was on display when He sent Jesus to conquer death and sin, die for us, and rise again, beating death. If we dive into this, it's better than any superhero story.

We mustn't be fooled. The enemy, the thief, is the destroyer of all good. Jesus is the healer and our daily hope in a really hard world.

Do I ever blame God when bad things happen? Why?

Instead, could I talk to God and invite Jesus into everything in my life?

We get to choose to invite Jesus in everyday, we need Him even when we don't realize it, He has come that we may have life to the FULL!

Jesus, remind me that You are for me, guard my thoughts and help me to choose You throughout each day. Protect me from the enemy. In Jesus name

What makes me smile?

1.
2.
3.
4.
5.

"My sheep recognize My voice. I know them and they follow Me. I give them real and eternal life. They are protected from the Destroyer for good. No one can steal them from out of my hand. The Father, who put them under My care is much greater than the Destroyer and the Thief. No one could ever get them away from Him." (John 10:30-32)

There *is* a destroyer. He seeks to wreck the good things in our life. He tries to make us think negatively about ourselves and others. He wants us to feel hopeless. He tries to convince us we are not lovable. He is also a thief, trying to steal our view of God and the best life He has for us. Not many of us like to talk about him. However, realizing that he is real and there is always a battle going on, for he is trying to ruin "life to the full," is important so we can equip ourselves to fight against him.

How do we work against him? We can realize that our negative thoughts about life, others, ourselves, and even God are not life-giving, but destructive. We can spend a few minutes every day in God's truth (the Bible) and we can invite Jesus into our thoughts throughout the day. God protects us from the destroyer. We must entrust ourselves to His care and listen to what He says about us!

Do I think destructive thoughts?

Can I trust God to take care of me and protect me from the enemy?

God, destructive thoughts are not from You. I give You all the negativity I think about. Help me to choose Your way of thinking. I give You me. I invite You into my thoughts and my moments, and my view of myself, others, and You. Protect me from the thief. In Jesus name

DAY 41

I love: (Here are a few of mine: I love laughter, moments with my kids, hikes with my husband, my siblings and our memories, my parents' encouragement, life-time friendships, our church, and the heart of God.)

1.
2.
3.
4.
5.

My youngest painted me a picture. To me it's a treasure, a modern-day Picasso. I believe God treasures our gifts to Him too. We may only see our mess ups or our imperfections, yet He sees our heart. He loves when we choose to give gifts to Him. Every word of encouragement, every act of kindness, every time we serve, every time we choose to pray instead of worry, every time we give joy, every time we share His heart, we give Him a gift.

What gift can I give to God?

The mystery of God amazes me, He fills our heart up with love and joy so we can give it away. The continual flow from His heart to ours is like a stream. His stream of love never runs dry, but continues to fill our hearts so that we can spill Him out.

"For God SO loved the world." (John 3:16 NIV) This includes you, me, those we love, and those who are hard to get along with... for He *"so loved"* everyone!

God, may Your love continually flow into my heart so that Your love flows out on others. In Jesus name

DAY 42

What is good in my life?

1.

2.

3.

4.

5.

This is the confidence we have in approaching God: that if we ask anything according to his will, he hears us. (1 John 5:14 NIV)

"There is so much simplicity in prayer."

"Jesus reminds us that prayer is a little like children coming to their parents. Our children come to us with the craziest requests at times! Often we are grieved by the meanness or selfishness in their requests, but we would be all the more grieved if they never came to us even in their meanness and selfishness. We are simply glad they do come—mixed motives and all.

This is precisely how it's with prayer. We will never have pure enough motives, or be good enough, or know enough in order to pray rightly. We simply must set all things aside and begin praying. In fact, it's the very act of prayer itself—the intimate, ongoing interaction with God—that these matters are cared for in due time. God receives us just the way we are and accepts our prayers just as they are." (Richard J. Foster, Prayer Finding the Heart's True Home)

Do I feel comfortable praying to God, because I know I am loved and accepted by Him?

God, this is what is on my mind _____. I invite You into this. In Jesus name

DAY 43

I am thankful for:

1.
2.
3.
4.
5.

"Now Jesus wept." (John 11:35 MSG)

Jesus knew He was about to do a miracle in this story. So why did He weep? Looking at the heart of God, I wonder if He wept because He entered the people's pain and grief. He felt their sadness, their loss, their hopelessness. Their pain became His pain.

Our closeness with God grows when we know and believe that He endures our pain with us. The rejection we feel, He feels it with us. The hurt we experience, He cries too. The anxiety we have, He comforts us. His heart anticipates the day when all will be right, no more sadness and no more tears. Until that day, he sits in our pain with us and offers us comfort.

Do I see God with me through my pain?

If not, what would change if I invited Him into my struggle?

God, thank You for weeping over loss and sadness. I invite You into my hurt, my struggle, my loss...heal my heart. Help me to see You as a God that enters my world and walks with me. In Jesus name

DAY 44

I am thankful for:

1.
2.
3.
4.
5.

"They were curious about Jesus." (John 12:55-56 MSG)

I love how people were *"curious"* about Jesus. I wonder what it felt like to be in the crowd listening to Him, watching Him dole out miracles, and seeing Him heal. I can imagine I would be curious. I hope that I would be more than curious, I hope I would have been captivated by his presence and followed Him everywhere. Would I have hung on every word He spoke? Would I be awed time and time again as He did miracles? Would I leave everything and follow Him? Or would I be skeptical and judgmental? (You can ask yourself these same questions.)

Two thousand years later, we can still wake up curious about Jesus. We can connect with Him by reading His Words, thinking about what we read, and inviting Him to lead us throughout the day. When we connect with Jesus, the love of Jesus recaptures our hearts over and over again, if we let it. His love is so big, it knows no boundaries.

God, show me more of You and the heart of Jesus. May Jesus lead me today in every area of my life. In Jesus name

What is good in my life?

1.
2.
3.
4.
5.

"It was because they had spread the word of this latest God-sign that the crowd swelled to a welcoming parade. The Pharisees took one look and threw up their hands: 'It's out of control. The world's in a stampede after him.'" (John 12:17-19 MSG)

There was always a crowd with Jesus. Many wanted healing, some wanted answers, others just wanted to be near Him. Yet there were also those set on rejecting Him. The Pharisees did not like all the attention He was getting, they didn't like the freedom He offered, and they were jealous. So they rejected Him.

We face rejection all the time. It doesn't feel good. When we get rejected it's hard to remember that it's probably more about the person rejecting us than it is about us. Maybe they are insecure or jealous. Rejection usually doesn't make sense, and it can be devastating, lonely, and even cruel.

Jesus felt this way too. He didn't do anything against this group of religious people who were set on rejecting Him. Their hate came at him out of fear and jealousy. Therefore, when we feel rejected we can find a safe place in His heart, giving this rejection to Him, for He understands exactly how it feels.

Who has rejected me? How does this affect my thoughts?

Can I give this to God?

God, I give You the rejection I have felt. Thank You for going through everything I feel here on Earth and understanding me. Heal my heart with Your great love. Wrap me in You. In Jesus name

DAY 46

What am I thankful for?

1.
2.
3.
4.
5.

"If any of you wants to serve me, then follow me. Then you'll be where I am, ready to serve at a moment's notice. The Father will honor and reward anyone who serves me." (John 12:26 MSG)

Serving is life-giving! It may sound like a chore or hard work, yet serving others creates inner joy and happiness. When we live self-absorbed, we can find so many things we wish were different in our world. We can be overly critical of ourselves and others. However, when we serve by helping someone else it makes us feel good too. Even though serving is not essentially about us, reaching out to others actually creates a positive impact in our heart! Serving can be as small as helping a parent or family member around the house, helping with younger children, reaching out to the elderly, taking time to encourage someone, getting involved in a ministry at church and so much more! We can live in an attitude of serving.

If we go about our life thinking, "you before me," we start to live out the example Jesus set for us. A "me first" mentality does not fulfill us on the inside, it leaves us wanting more. When we come alongside the heart of God by serving we feel satisfied and at peace.

Who can I serve today?

God, help me to look outside myself and serve someone who needs Your love. Help me to live in an attitude of service, choosing you before me. In Jesus name

DAY 47

What can I celebrate?

1.
2.
3.
4.
5.

"Jesus said, 'Father, glorify your name!' Then a voice came from heaven, 'I have glorified it, and will glorify it again.' The crowd that was there and heard it said it had thundered; others said an angel had spoken to him. Jesus said, 'This voice was for your benefit, not mine. Now is the time for judgment on this world; now the prince of this world will be driven out. And I, when I am lifted up from the earth, will draw all people to myself.'" (John 12:28-32 NIV)

Hearing a voice from Heaven would be amazing! If God spoke to us in an audible voice from above, what would we want to hear? Maybe an answer to a problem we have been dealing with, or maybe we would want to hear that everything is going to be okay. Perhaps we would want to be reminded how much He loves us.

When we read in the Bible, we are reading His voice and His words. He speaks things like, "You are a masterpiece, my special treasure. I know the plans I have for you, plans to prosper you. I (Jesus) have come so that you will have life to the full."

He speaks amazing things to us that we can think about continually. His words will become the echo in our mind, which will give us a life of hope, enjoyment, and peace.

Do I listen to what God's voice tells me from the truths in Scripture?

God, I want to hear You. Help me to focus on Your truths. In Jesus name

What are five things I'm good at?

1.
2.
3.
4.
5.

"Give your entire attention to what God is doing right now, and don't get worked up about what may or may not happen tomorrow. God will help you deal with whatever hard things come up when the time comes." (Matthew 6:34 MSG)

Early this morning, God started whispering to me, "faith...or fear?"

We have a choice. To be set apart in our faith, we have to risk, to trust, to choose faith over our fears. There will always be things we can choose to fear in every area of our lives: school, work, our economy, politics, future opportunities, our dreams, health and more. Through all of that, we can still trust in God and rely on Him.

We can choose faith, because of these truths about God:
God loves us.

He sent Jesus to deliver us from sin by living a perfect and blameless life and then dying for our failures so we could live in freedom. Nothing can separate us from God's love.

We can choose to live in faith even if we don't feel like it. When do I not feel like choosing faith?
We can put our trust in Jesus, which may feel like a risk, yet it will change everything in amazing ways and give us the courage to live out our faith.

Jesus, I believe YOU are for me, You died for me, You rose again. I choose to trust You, even when I don't feel like it. I invite Your love and power into my life.

DAY 49

What is good in my life?

1.
2.
3.
4.
5.

"When you come to him, that fullness comes together for you, too. His power extends over everything." (Colossians 2:10 MSG)

After it rains the ground is soft and muddy, puddles are covering the roads. When the ground is soft like that, it's easy for water to slip through the cracks and fill up the holes. God reminded me that His love saturates our hearts just like the water soaking into the ground. Our heart can find a safe place in His love. Like a sponge, we can soak it in and when it runs dry, His love pours down on us again to fill up our heart. There is a constant downpour from His heart to ours. Living immersed in His love is life to the FULLEST!

So how do we live this out practically? Every single day is full of ups and downs. If we have a God-centered "go to" that echoes in our head, we can live confident and secure in that. A "go to" thought is a repetitive idea that centers us continually throughout the day, when life is good and also when it is hard.

Here's an example, "I am radically loved by God, this defines who I am, I invite Jesus into this situation." We can live in the downpour of God's love by being aware and thinking positive and uplifting thoughts like this.

What can be my "go to" thought?

God, I invite You to remind me throughout the day that Your love is my security, my confidence, my home. In Jesus name

Good things in my life:

1.
2.
3.
4.
5.

"Jesus said, 'For a brief time still, the light is among you. Walk by the light you have so darkness doesn't destroy you. If you walk in darkness, you don't know where you're going. As you have the light, believe in the light. Then the light will be within you, and shining through your lives. You'll be children of light.'" (John 12:35-36 MSG)

Walking in the light sounds simple, yet it isn't always easy in a world where there are a lot of dark areas. Being aware of where you are walking and avoiding grey areas is the key to not finding yourself stuck in the dark, without realizing how you got there. Maybe you are in a season where some of those things in the "darkness," like parties, gossiping, and unhealthy friendships or choices might sound fun, but with the darkness comes regret and the potential for heartache. So how do we know how to "stay in the light?"

Spending a few minutes each day with God invites His light into our lives. Walking in that light means being constantly aware that as believers, He has called us to something different, something better! If we have a relationship with God, we can bring His light everywhere we go by the way we treat others, the things we post, the choices we make, the words we say, and the thoughts we think. We get to choose. Walking in the light is life-giving! When you are consciously walking in the light, you remove yourself from situations that would make it all too easy to fall into a bad habit or a situation.

Are the choices I'm making leading me to light or to darkness?

God, sometimes it's hard to avoid darkness. Help me. Give me strength to make decisions that would lead me to Your light. In Jesus name

What are some small things I am thankful for?

1.
2.
3.
4.
5.

"All of these God-signs he had given them and they still didn't get it, still wouldn't trust Him." (John 12:12 MSG)

"God-signs." If we look around we can see them everywhere. A sunrise, an answered prayer, a kind or encouraging word, a great moment, something that makes us laugh, progress and so many others. We can see little God-signs and big, amazing God-signs. Seeing these signs and being aware of them changes our perspective. We can either focus on the overwhelming life stuff or the signs He shows us every day. Focusing on what God is doing creates happiness and provides hope.

What are some God-signs in your life?

God, help me to see Your hand through the good and bad. You are always doing life with me and You are always there for me. Remind me of this. In Jesus name

DAY 52

Who are people I enjoy?

1.
2.
3.
4.
5.

We have people in our life who make us smile, people who we love doing life with and we always enjoy!

"By yourself you're unprotected. With a friend you can face the worst. Can you round up a third? A three-stranded rope isn't easily snapped." (Ecclesiastes 4:12 MSG)

We need friends, we were not meant to figure life out by ourselves. Friends can make us better spiritually, mentally, and in all aspects of our life. Friends and even mentors can be gifts that God places in our life. On the flip side, we can be a great friend to others and help them become their best self.

Do you have a friend that encourages you to be a better you?

God, show me who in my life will encourage me to grow and show me who I can reach out to and be a friend. I invite You into all my relationships. In Jesus name

What is good in my life?

1.
2.
3.
4.
5.

"Do not let your hearts be troubled. Trust in God; trust also in Me (Jesus)." (John 14:1 NIV)

Researchers have discovered that we can think up to 60,000 thoughts a day. We are *always* thinking. All too often, we can get stuck in the thoughts that trouble us:
What does my future look like?
How do I navigate this situation?
What are my options?
How should I respond?
What's next?

Life is full of moments of greatness and laughter; conversely, life is also full of situations that surprise us, disappoint us, and sometimes, devastate us. Sometimes, our response to this can be unclear. We just don't know what to do.

When our hearts are troubled, we can CHOOSE to trust in God (Jesus). We can trust that His heart for us is good and He will help us. We can replay the troubles over and over again in our minds OR we can think prayers to God. Thinking about the "what if's" and other negative thoughts can ruin our day, but spending time thinking about God's love gives us hope. Although this isn't easy, we get to choose what we think about.

What is bothering me?

How can I turn my thoughts toward Jesus?

God, I give You _____ (all the stuff that I worry about and get consumed with). Please help me know what to do, I choose to trust You with all of this. Please provide in amazing ways! In Jesus name

DAY 54

Good things in my life:

1.
2.
3.
4.
5.

"Jesus told him, 'I am the way, the truth, and the life. No one can come to the Father except through me.'" (John 14:6 NLT)

Real life is found in connecting with God. Most of us at some point have searched for something to make us feel better. However, physical things will never fill the hunger in our souls to connect with God through a relationship with Jesus. We are much more complex than we realize. The physical and worldly has limitations, but the spiritual quenches a hunger in our souls that nothing else can fill. This mystery astounds me. Taking moments to connect with God by reading a Bible verse, thinking about how it applies, inviting God into all of our life situations, and thanking Him for the good creates life to the fullest regardless of our circumstances.

What do I turn to in an attempt to fill an inner hunger?

Does this keep me full?

Jesus, You are the Source of Life. Real life is found in connecting with You. Show me Your Way and the Truth of Who You are. In Your name

What is good in my life?

1.
2.
3.
4.
5.

"If you love me, keep my commands." (John 14:15 NIV)

Why do we do the right thing? When I understood this verse, it changed my walk with God.

Every time we choose to do the right thing we are showing God that we love Him. He *is* love, it's His entire essence. Nothing can take us away from His love. He loves us regardless of our choices! However, He longs for us to choose the right thing, because He knows the heartache darkness leaves in its wake.

So, when we choose not to go there, say that, send that, take that (fill in the blank) we are saying, "God, I love You, I choose You." We can express our gratitude and love to God by choosing to do the right thing. He knows we will not get it perfect and He promises to help us.

What am I wrestling with?

Have I invited God to help me? Why or Why not?

God, I want to choose the right thing. Forgive my wrong choices. Help me to follow Your way. Thank You for loving me with a never-ending love. In Jesus name

DAY 56

What is great in my life?

1.
2.
3.
4.
5.

"Now I'm turning you over to God, our marvelous God whose gracious Word can make you into what he wants you to be and give you everything you could possibly need in this community of holy friends." (Acts 20:32 MSG)

If we wake up every morning and think, "It's gonna be a great day," regardless of our situation, something great will happen! Even on those worst days, we can wake up and look for the good in our day. That is one of the first things I tell myself in the morning because our thoughts jumpstart our brain and shape our life!

What if your first thought was not, "Oh no, I have this," or, "Oh no, I am dreading that," or, "I wish I was…" Instead, what if we woke up and thought, "Today is going to be a great day!"

To keep this attitude throughout the day, we could choose to think or whisper a quiet prayer every time a worry or unknown pops into our head, "Lord I trust You to take care of _____."

Today is going to be a great day, if we choose it! Our attitude about life affects everything. How can we take this greatness throughout our day? We can live wrapped in God's love, we can give life to others, which makes us feel happier, and we can continue to work on and improve the things in our current situation (school, work, sports, music, drama, future goals).

Jesus, I trust Your heart for me I choose to. Even when it doesn't feel like it's gonna be a great day, I choose to believe You are for me and You are working something great! In Your name

DAY 57

Five great things in my life:

1.
2.
3.
4.
5

"Praise him from sunrise to sunset!" (Psalms 113:3 TLB)

What would change if I whispered this simple prayer throughout the day? "Jesus, I invite you into...this conversation, this class or meeting, this moment with my friends or family, my routine, my plans, my to do list, my hopes and dreams, everything!" What if I tried this for 24 hours? What would change? What if I tried this for a whole week?

For me this would mean waking up and inviting Jesus into my exercise routine, conversations with my family, my drive on the way to school and work, my thoughts on how to care for others that week, my meetings, my moments of brainstorming, dinner time, what I do with some free time, and my thoughts before I go to sleep.

What would this look like for you?

What would change if we invited the presence and power of Jesus into our moments, our thoughts, and every interaction we have?

Let's try it and take some notes on how we feel and the unexpected things God does in our lives.

Jesus, I invite You into _____.

DAY 58

Things I am thankful for:

1.
2.
3.
4.
5.

"These things I have spoken to you while I am still with you. But the Helper, the Holy Spirit, whom the Father will send in my name, he will teach you all things and bring to your remembrance all that I have said to you. Peace I leave with you; my peace I give to you. Not as the world gives do I give to you. Let not your hearts be troubled, neither let them be afraid." (John 14:25-27 ESV)

God is with us in the form of the Holy Spirit. The Spirit, although much more powerful, is like the air we breath. Even though we can not see Him, He is always there. When we spend time with God, we get more peaceful. Have you ever met those people who shine with God's joy and radiate peace and love?

Who in my life is like this?

Those are people who intentionally spend time with God and embrace His Holy Spirit. This is an amazing mystery. His Spirit speaks to ours, quenching a need we didn't know existed.

The world gives us lots of stress, anxiety, and fears, but we don't have to just accept it. We can choose to spend a few minutes talking to God, reading a verse, journaling about what we think it means. This practice changes our inner self and guides us down a journey of peace.

God, I invite Your Spirit to teach me new things, fill me with Your peace, and speak to my heart. In Jesus name

What good things do I enjoy?

1.
2.
3.
4.
5.

"If anyone hears what I am saying and doesn't take it seriously, I don't reject him. I didn't come to reject the world; I came to save the world. But you need to know that whoever puts me off, refusing to take in what I'm saying, is willfully choosing rejection." (John 12:47 MSG)

Can you think of a time when you were rejected?

I can. It stinks, it didn't feel good! I can look back and remember friends who rejected me, my high school boyfriend who dumped me, competitions where I wasn't chosen...the list goes on. The world is full of rejection, but God is not. He, *"didn't come to reject the world."* He wants us to accept Him and rest in the thought that we have already been accepted by Him. I have often thought about how He felt when he was rejected. I can imagine it broke His heart much more deeply than a high school breakup or a friend's rebuff.

We get to choose to accept Him and His gift of love and total acceptance.

Jesus, I accept Your great love for me. I give You the times I have felt rejected and the hurt this caused, please heal my heart and mind from this. I choose to forgive this person who rejected me _____. Help me to show acceptance to others. In Jesus name

What can I be thankful for amidst the unknowns?

1.
2.
3.
4.
5.

"I have told you these things, so that in me (Jesus) you may have peace. In this world you will have trouble. But take heart! I have overcome the world." (John 13:33 NIV)

For the next 30 days, I will be writing about PEACE. So many of us either currently struggle with or have struggled with anxiety. In all of the unknowns, we can still choose peace. There are so many unknowns and we might be worried about our loved ones or ourselves.

The solution to our anxiety, fear of the unknown, and worry for others is in Jesus. With Him, we can have peace. This verse does not say, "life will be perfect or completely mapped out." It just promises peace, regardless of our circumstances.

Practically, what does this look like? Each time we feel restless, whispering or thinking a prayer, inviting Jesus into our worry, our unknowns, our disappointments, our fears, our negative thoughts or downward spiral.

Jesus, I invite You into ALL of the thoughts that are swirling in my brain. I choose to trust You in the midst of unknowns. Please give me Your unexplainable peace in Your name.

DAY 61

I am thankful for:

1.
2.
3.
4.
5.

"And now [brethren], I commit you to God [I deposit you in His charge, entrusting you to His protection and care]. And I commend you to the Word of His grace [to the commands and counsels and promises of His unmerited favor]. It is able to build you up and to give you [your rightful] inheritance among all God's set-apart ones (those consecrated, purified, and transformed of soul)." (Acts 20:32 AMPC)

We can use this verse as a prayer by saying, "And now _____ (my troubles, frustration, anxiety about something, fear, whatever it is for you), I commit you to God..."

We can ask ourselves:
What are things I need to entrust to Him today?
What do I fear when it comes to change?

What do I worry about?
What is a dream God placed in my heart?
What do I hope for someone that I love?

By surrendering these desires daily and giving them to God, He in exchange gives us His peace.

God, I give You my worries, my hopes, dreams, needs, worries… everything! I give You me. I invite Jesus into every area of my life. As I entrust things into your care, please give me Your peace. In Jesus name

What is good in my life?

1.
2.
3.
4.
5.

"Do not fear for I am with you, do not be dismayed for I am your God. I will strengthen and help you, I will uphold you with my righteous right hand." (Isaiah 41:1 NIV)

The storms of life rage around us sometimes. Life is not always calm, calculated, and predictable. We can make guesses to how things will turn out, or talk about what could happen, but no one really knows the future. This made me think back to an unpredictable and unexpected storm that my daughter and I were caught in a few years ago. She and I were outside at a sporting event and without warning lightning bolts ignited through the sky, the beautiful day turned dangerous within a couple of minutes. In fear and helplessness, we were caught outside surrounded by water. The storm came so quickly and we couldn't get to the car safely.

I said a prayer. Instead of the storm easing up, it erupted with deafening thunder and threatening lightning.

After about ten minutes I thought, "How can I protect my daughter in this storm?" Then I realized I couldn't, only God could. The storm was right above us. Lightning hit an object nearby. During this half hour I have never felt so helpless and, in an odd way, secure. I knew life was totally out of my control, but God's shield was my hope for my daughter and me. Later in the evening I was shaky as the "what ifs" taunted my mind. There was no way for me to work harder to fix this storm and I couldn't manipulate it. I was solely reliant on the Maker *and* Calmer of all storms.

Have you ever felt that way? You are on the other side of the storm, yet you can't help but spiral into thoughts of what *could* have happened. Here are some questions to reflect on if you find yourself in that type of situation.

In what ways can I give God control through this storm?

What negative thoughts can I relinquish to Him?

In giving Him our storms, we can greet life with peacefulness.

Jesus, please shield me and my family from the storm raging around us. Help me to choose to look to You and Your might, instead of the storm. In Jesus name

DAY 63

What can I do today?

1.
2.
3.
4.
5.

"Oh give thanks to the Lord." (Psalms 107:1 ESV)

It is easy to thank God when everything is going well, it is much harder to thank Him when life is difficult. As I write, we are in 2020, this has been a hard year. Because of the epidemic, there are so many things that changed or won't look the same for a long time. It's easy to feel hopeless, confused, frustrated or mad. In contrast, if we want to enjoy life, we can think about what we CAN do today. We can choose to think of the positive experiences we still have every day. We can think great, we can encourage someone around us, we can be kind, we can learn something new, we can work on our dreams, we can make someone's life better by the way we treat them.

What can I do today to reach out to someone else?

If you feel stuck because of the ways something out of your control is affecting your life, the truth is, you aren't stuck. Even if it feels like life is falling apart, you can choose to look outside your own circumstances and give life to someone else by your words and actions. A bonus of serving others is that it usually brings you joy and makes you feel better too!

God, I wrestle with disappointment over all the things I can't do right now, I give You this feeling. Change my focus on what I can do today to make someone else's day better. In Jesus name

Five things good in my life:

1.
2.
3.
4.
5.

"Save me, God, for the water has risen to my neck. I have sunk in deep mud, and there is no footing; I have come into deep water, and a flood sweeps over me. I am weary from my crying; my throat is parched. My eyes fail, looking for my God." (Psalm 69:1-3 CSB)

If our thoughts start spiraling with all of the negatives and the disappointments, we can feel overwhelmed, depressed, or anxious. It's easy to either stay in those melancholy feelings, or ignore them all together. However, allowing yourself to stay down or ignoring your feelings doesn't make them go away.

Facing the truth helps us move on. Try this four-step process to help you the next time you feel overwhelmed or anxious:

Take a moment and write down all of the yuck surrounding what you are feeling or going through. Your disappointments, your frustrations, your fears, the *real* stuff. Writing these things down helps us own them and it takes away the power for them to affect our emotions. Facing the real helps us to move on. This may sound silly, but I call this, "Sitting in the mud puddle." You may feel like you are sinking into the mud, or you don't have solid ground to stand on, but after sitting in this and writing these things down, we can decide to move on.

Getting out of the mud starts with giving all of these thoughts to God. "God, I give You all of this disappointment, sadness, worry, anger, loneliness, and (fill in the blank) _____. Please take this from me and give me Your peace, joy, and love instead. In Jesus name."

In every season there may be difficulties around us, but we can thank God for the good. Thanking God for the good blesses Him, but it also does something in us. It helps our thoughts focus on the positive rather than the negative. Thanking God for the good gives us hope. *"I will praise God's name in song and glorify him with thanksgiving." (Psalm 69:30 NIV).* Earlier in this passage David talks about sinking and feeling stuck, but even through that he finishes the Psalm by praying and thanking God.

We can reach out to someone. Sometimes it feels a little hard to reach out to someone or to know how to start the conversation, but we can text, facetime, or call a friend. I guarantee that someone else needs your friendship today.

God, remind me that You are good and that You are for me, remind me that there are things to be thankful for. Show me who to reach out to. In Jesus name

What five things am I thankful for?

1.
2.
3.
4.
5.

"Trust in the Lord with all your heart, and do not rely on your own understanding. Acknowledge him in all your ways, and he will make your paths straight." (Proverbs 3:5-6 NET)

The coffee mug I most look forward to using every morning has the word "trust" written on it in big letters along with the rest of this verse. I got stuck on the word "acknowledge." What does it mean to acknowledge? And how does that relate to God?

To "acknowledge" is to, "admit to be real or true; recognize the existence, truth, or fact; to recognize the authority, validity, or claims of; show or express appreciation or gratitude for; take notice of, or reply to." (dictionary.com)

Part of acknowledging God means to admit He is real, recognize Him and His authority, appreciate Him, and to reply to Him.

If I just thought about the first definition, "admit He is real," what would this mean for me?

God *is* real. He is love, He is the Creator, He cares about me, He made me, He knows me and loves me. How does knowing this change my thoughts about life and myself?

God, I realize that You are God, You love me, You sent Your Son to rescue me. I want to recognize You throughout my day every day. In Your name

DAY 66

What is good in my life?

1.

2.

3.

4.

5.

Am I thriving or surviving?

Every moment, we get a choice to live getting better or getting bitter, even in a difficult situation or season. Our attitude does not have to be dependent on our circumstances. We can feel overwhelmed or anxious, but we do not have to live this out.

"He explained everything about Jesus Christ. His door was always open." *(Acts 28:31 MSG)*

There is this crazy story in the Bible in the book of Acts (verses 27-28). Paul was taken prisoner for following Jesus. He is in a 14 day storm, and then he is stuck on an Island for three months. He didn't deserve it, and it certainly wasn't fair. Yet, he chose to thrive in this unfortunate situation anyway, and he found ways to make the lives of those around him better too. In a tough season we can ask ourselves:

Will I come out of this better?

Will the people I'm around be better because of me?

How can I bring life to others?

How can I still thrive?

Life as we know it can be different. Yet, we are not bound to the way we *feel* like reacting. We can give life to others. We can spend time with God daily. We can find creative ways to work on ourselves and get better at the things we enjoy. We can be kind to the people we are living with. We get to *choose* to thrive and to help others around us thrive.

Jesus, I invite You into my situation, my thoughts, my disappointments, my boredom, my frustration, my fears, my feelings of _____. I want to thrive. Show me how to live life to the FULL and give life to others each day. In Jesus name

DAY 67

What can I be thankful for today:

1.
2.
3.
4.
5.

"I (Jesus) give you a new command: Love one another." (John 13:34 MSG)

It can be difficult to show love to the people we are living with. Sometimes it is easier to be loving or kind to a friend, or even an acquaintance. Our family can be the most difficult ones to be kind and loving to. Why? Maybe it's because we are familiar with them. Maybe because we expect more out of them. Maybe because they annoy us. Maybe because we take them for granted. Maybe because we just don't feel like it.

Many years ago something changed my perspective on this. I facilitated a group for high school students who had lost a sibling or parent. They lived in so much regret for things they said or didn't say while their family members were around. I learned so much from them. Siblings can be our biggest gift if we let them.

How can I give life to the people around me (in my home)?

Every moment, we can choose our actions and our words. We can choose to be kind to those around us, whether or not we feel like they deserve it.

God, help me to show love to the people I am at home with. Forgive me for the times I have been unkind. Help me to choose my words even when I don't feel like it. In Jesus name

I am thankful for:

1.
2.
3.
4.
5.

"Live freely animated and motivated by God's Spirit. Then you won't feed the compulsions of selfishness." (Galatians 5:16-17 MSG)

To live freely—don't we all want that? It's hard to feel free or motivated when there is a negative swirl in our minds. One thing that can rob us from living freely is when someone hurts our feelings and we replay it in our minds over and over again. Most of us do this without realizing it. We say we're fine or we don't care, but inside we keep thinking about the hurtful words that were said. This morning, I was doing this and God whispered, "Thinking about this will not bring joy, happiness, or allow you to have a great day." Immediately, we can change our thoughts, but if we don't deal with and process the thought or hurt, it will come back.

To get rid of nagging hurtful thoughts, we can:

1. Acknowledge it. (This person's words bothered me.)
2. Choose to forgive them. (Saying a prayer about this is most powerful.)
3. Confront them. (Seek wise counsel first.)
4. Reroute your mind to think about a positive. (Every time the hurt is replayed, think about something life-giving.)
5. Remind ourselves we already forgave the person!

Is something someone did or said bothering you?

Can you choose to deal with this thought?

Life to the full is available to all of us!

God, I can't stop thinking about _____. I give this thought to You, I choose to forgive _____. Please forgive my bitterness toward them. I don't want to let this thought have any power over me, so I give it to You. In Jesus name

DAY 69

What are five small things I enjoy?

1.
2.
3.
4.
5.

"But Jesus said, 'Let the children come to me. Don't stop them! For the Kingdom of Heaven belongs to those who are like these children.'" (Matthew 19:14 NLT)

God wants us to be like children, this simplifies life and our relationship with God. Children trust easily, but sometimes we, as teens or adults, doubt or hold back. Maybe a past pain has made us jaded, but most children live free from the restraints of self-doubts or fears. Simplicity is freeing! We don't have to be more, do more, have more, or work harder to be close to God, we can simply say prayers like this throughout the day, "I give everyone and everything to you, God" (John Eldredge, Get Your Life Back).

This goes along with inviting Jesus into everything. We can give every worry, every test, every project, every failure, every stressful moment, every interaction...every single moment to God. This takes the stress off of us and gives us life to the full! I encourage you to try it!

Is there anything that I have a hard time giving to God?

God, I give _____ (everything on my mind) and _____ (everyone on my mind) to You. In Jesus name

I am thankful for:

1.
2.
3.
4.
5.

"Thank God no matter what happens." (1 Thessalonians 5:18 MSG)

What? No matter what happens? There are no "buts" or "ifs" here, just...be thankful always! God knew if we chose thankful thoughts we would live a happier life. When we take the time to think about our thankfuls, our mood changes, we gain a new perspective, and we enjoy life more.

Even during hard or confusing seasons, we can think of things we are thankful for. Why? Living thankful makes us better. Living thankful fights depression and anxiety. Living thankful is motivating. Living thankful makes us more fun to be around.

In college I ran marathons. One of my best friends and running partner, Tobi, reminded me to choose thankfulness. After 15 mile runs, I would complain about my legs and she would laugh and say, "Just be thankful you have legs and can run." I think about her words every time I am sore from working out. Being sore reminds me to be thankful that I am able to go on runs.

Do I live thankful?

We can find things to be thankful about, which will give us life to the fullest.

God, when I think negatively, remind me of the good things in my life. I invite You into every aspect of my life. In Jesus name

DAY 71

What am I thankful for?

1.
2.
3.
4.
5.

"Since this is the kind of life we have chosen, the life of the Spirit... That means we will not compare ourselves with each other as if one of us were better and another worse. We have far more interesting things to do with our lives. Each of us is an original." (Galatians 5:25-26 MSG)

When we compare ourselves to others, it steals our joy. Sometimes we compare ourselves without even realizing it. We can usually find someone better and worse in every area. Competing in a world of achievers is hard. We have a tendency to wonder if we measure up. This verse says, *"We have far more interesting things to do with our lives. Each of us is an original."* God made us all originals, none of us are the exact same and none of us have the same God-given gifts, adventures, and dreams. So, comparing ourselves is a waste of time.

What does the best version of me look like?

How do I become the best version of me?

What God-given gifts and talents do I have that will be life-giving to others?

How can I be the best version of me even when I am facing difficult challenges?

God, thank You for making me an original. Stop my thoughts when they want to go in a negative direction and compare myself to others. I invite You into every aspect of my life. In Jesus name

I am thankful for:

1.
2.
3.
4.
5.

"Go after a life of love as if your life depended on it—because it does."
(1 Corinthians 14:1 MSG)

There are a lot of verses about waiting and being still, but this one says, "GO!" It's talking about love. This verse has many dimensions. First, we must accept the love of God. He loves us to the core of our being. He loves us in our broken and messy, and in our great and thriving. The God of the Universe loves us with a love that knows no limits no boundaries. His love is big and sturdy enough to place our entire self-worth on. When we ask ourselves, "Do I measure up?" We can answer this question with, "I have worth because the God of the Universe made me and loves me." All the extras (titles, awards, achievements, compliments) are like icing on a cake, but a strong foundation to base our life on is found in the love of God.

How do we *"go after a life of love?"*
1. Everyday, when we wake up we can remind ourselves of God's great love for us.
2. When lies about our worth pop into our minds, we can stop and change those thoughts replacing them with what God says about us.
   (Side note: There are so many verses in the Bible about what God says about us, "Masterpiece, treasure, royalty, His sons and daughters.)
3. We can constantly give His love to others.

We can always choose to go after a life of love!

God, show me what it means to base my worth in Your love, and to go after a life of love. I invite Jesus to change my negative thoughts about me. Show me who to reach out to today.

DAY 73

I woke up thankful for:

1.
2.
3.
4.
5.

"I'm bankrupt without love, love never gives up." *(1 Corinthians 13:7 MSG)*

The Source of love (God) never gives up. He pursues us, forgives us, gives us hope, and promises peace. His love for us is like a never ending river flowing from His heart to ours. It's where that inner thirst is quenched. Nothing else fills us, our hearts were made to be continually filled with His love.

It's easy to try to fill up our schedules with fun things. We can hope that movies, video games, social media and other people will either give us hope, or numb us to what's really going on. All these things are fun, yet all of these leave us unsatisfied and wanting more.

How am I doing today? Am I thirsty for something?

God's love is constantly pursuing us. His love can drive out hopelessness and sadness. Living in Him is key in every season.

We can wake up and spend a few minutes with God, remind ourselves throughout the day that He is with us and for us, and whisper a prayer of thanks before we go to sleep. We can live full when we choose to live aware of God throughout the day. We can live full of His love, regardless of our circumstances.

God, I choose to live in Your love. Saturate my heart with Your love and hope. Remind me that Your love is the Source of life. I give You me. In Jesus name

What am I thankful for?

1.
2.
3.
4.
5.

"Trust in the Lord with all your heart and lean not on your own understanding; in all your ways submit to him, and he will make your paths straight." (Proverbs 3:5-6 NIV)

Personalizing Scripture helps us grow in our walk with God. One way to do this is to read a verse and ask ourselves questions about it. For instance, in this verse we can ask:

Do I trust that God is for me and loves me?

What part of my heart am I not trusting God with (my future, this situation, a relationship)?

What do I fear could happen?

Will I invite God into my situation by praying and submitting it to Him?

Will I follow His way for me?

When we break apart a verse by asking ourselves questions, we face our thoughts and we can be real with God. God loves us completely. He also already knows us inside and out, so our answers don't surprise Him. We get to choose to trust Him, to let go of our own way of dealing with things, to submit to Him, and ask Him to show us the way.

God, help me to trust you no matter what. Even when I am facing something new or unknown, help me to trust that Your heart for me is good, which leads me to give You control. Show me Your way for me. In Jesus name.

DAY 75

What is great in my life?

1.

2.

3.

4.

5.

"Summing it all up, friends, I'd say you'll do best by filling your minds and meditating on things true, noble, reputable, authentic, compelling, gracious—the best, not the worst; the beautiful, not the ugly; things to praise, not things to curse." (Philippians 4:8)

Sometimes I don't know what to think. Some things feel very surreal or far away. In contrast, hearing heartbreaking stories feels too hard or scary. With all of this, we can just feel numb. In this verse, we are given a solution. To think about: *"The best, not the worst; the beautiful, not the ugly; things to praise, not things to curse."*

It is helpful to make a list of great moments during a hard time. Whatever the situation, we can create great memories. In this chapter, Paul tells us he has the recipe for happiness. Much of this has to do with what we are thinking about.

What are you thinking about?

What are some great moments you can remember?

What are some great moments we can have today?

God, here are all of the negatives I'm feeling. Please help me to choose to think about the good things. Give me energy to make great moments during all times. In Jesus name

Good things in my life:

1.
2.
3.
4.
5.

"My counsel is this: Live freely, animated and motivated by God's Spirit. Then you won't feed the compulsions of selfishness. For there is a root of sinful self-interest in us that is at odds with a free spirit, just as the free spirit is incompatible with selfishness...so that you cannot live at times one way and at times another way according to how you feel on any given day. Why don't you choose to be led by the Spirit." (Galatians 5:16-18 MSG)

Have you realized that on any given day our emotions can be all over the place? There are days when it feels like we are riding a roller coaster. But even when we are experiencing twists and turns, we don't have to let our feelings tell us what to do. Instead, we can invite God's Spirit to help us. We can acknowledge what we are feeling or facing and then give it to Him. Then we can choose to let God's peace and hope guide us. For example, "God,

I feel so disappointed about _____. I am bothered by
_____. Please fill me with Your hope and light my
path." Then go reach out to someone or do something nice for
another person.

We are not stuck in whatever we are feeling, we can choose to
let His Spirit lead us!

God, fill me with Your love, joy, and hope today. All day long
remind me to choose my thoughts wisely. Show me who to reach
out to today. In Jesus name

DAY 77

What are five great things in my life?

1.
2.
3.
4.
5.

"Cast all your anxiety on Him, because He cares for you." (1 Peter 5:7 NIV)

Have you ever gone fishing? This verse always makes me think about it. Something about being around the water is so peaceful. When we throw the line out, we cast it far away from us. This verse never tells us to reel our anxieties back in, simply cast them out and leave it there.

What anxieties do I need to cast to God?

Anxieties take many different forms, worries about our health or finances, worries about a family member, worries about the future, worries about a dream or goal, fear of the unknown. Sometimes, we don't even know what we are anxious about, we just feel unsettled in our core. When we cast these things on God, He promises to give us His peace in exchange. We get to choose to accept His gift of inner peace.

God, I am anxious about _____. Here are all the things that swirl in my mind. I give them to You. Please give me Your peace instead. In Jesus name

How am I growing?

1.
2.
3.
4.
5.

"Grow in grace and understanding of our Master and Savior, Jesus Christ." (2 Peter 3:18 MSG)

We get to choose to grow and learn from everything we face. Sometimes it's hard to get started, but growing and bettering ourselves is motivating. How can we come out of every situation a better version of ourselves? How can we grow and learn from the obstacles we overcome? Most of the people who we read about in the Bible did not have it easy, yet their life situation made them stronger and better.

Doing a few small things can be super powerful. Take a few minutes to reflect on these questions:
What is one thing I can do to grow in my walk with God?

What is one thing I can do to be healthier today?
What is one thing I can do to be more active?
What is one way I can work on my hobby or dream?
What is one way I can help or encourage someone else?

Growing and thriving in tough situations is life giving! We can choose to be the best version of ourselves regardless of what we are going through.

God, I want to grow and thrive, empower me with Your Spirit. When I don't feel like doing small things to grow, help me, give me Your strength. Help me to come out of every situation better. In Jesus name

DAY 79

What am I grateful for:

1.
2.
3.
4.
5.

"God's Spirit touches our spirits and confirms who we really are. We know who he is, and we know who we are: Father and children. And we know we are going to get what's coming to us—an unbelievable inheritance! We go through exactly what Christ goes through." (Romans 8:12-14 MSG)

When I was in high school I didn't know the power of thoughts. Life was centered around performance in school, sports, competitions, and academics. When I look back, my negative thoughts were defeating all of the hours of work I was putting in. Why do we do this?

Most of us don't realize that we are defeating ourselves in our thoughts. We can ask ourselves:
What do I say to myself in my own head?

What do I tell myself when I look in the mirror?
Would I treat someone I care about the way I treat myself in my thoughts?

I recently had a conversation with a student who was doing this. I told her, "You are amazing and so dedicated, but you are constantly defeating yourself. It would be like this, doing something to better yourself—studying for a test, working out or, practicing your hobby—and afterward beating yourself up, mentally thinking negative thoughts about yourself. It's like you're punching yourself over and over again. This does not benefit you and all the hard work you just put in. You are too amazing to continue doing this."

Performance and thoughts coincide. We live out our thoughts in every area of our life. "If you realized how powerful your thoughts are, you would never think a negative thought." (Caroline Leaf, Switch on Your Brain). We can choose our thoughts, they don't choose us. God wants us to think good about ourselves, because He created us and loves us with an all-consuming love.

God, here are all of the negative thoughts I think about me. I give them to You. Stop me when I am beating myself up with my thoughts. Help me to think of me the way You do. You call me a masterpiece, chosen, daughter or son, treasure, more than a conqueror. Help me to tell myself the same messages. In Jesus name

DAY 80

I am thankful for:

1.
2.
3.
4.
5.

"In every situation, by prayer and petition, with thanksgiving, present your requests to God." (Philippians 4:6 NIV)

Why, "with thanksgiving?" When we thank God it blesses Him. It also does something in us. Thanking God makes us aware of what He is doing, what He has done, and His goodness. When we thank God, we are changed. We feel hopeful and happier.

What in my life makes it hard for me to choose to be thankful? Why?

One reason to start every day with five thankfuls or five great things is because being thankful changes our mind and can actually physically change the health of our brain. Thanking God is one of the best things we can do!

Thank You, God for _____. In Jesus name

DAY 81

I am thankful for:

1.
2.
3.
4.
5.

"May the God of hope fill you with JOY and PEACE as you trust Him, so that you may overflow with hope by the power of the Holy Spirit." *(Romans 15:13 NIV)*

When I think of overflowing, I picture pouring a cup of water until it is full and continuing to pour as the water spills everywhere. Or a rushing waterfall, and how beautiful and powerful it looks.

Overflowing with hope during a difficult time, sounds impossible, doesn't it? There are so many unknowns. We can feel out of control with what's going on around us. We can let this overwhelm us to the point where we feel hopeless, or we can choose to trust God regardless of our current circumstances. Trust is not a feeling, it's a choice. Throughout the day we are flooded with a roller coaster of feelings. We can start the day great, but doubting thoughts can taunt us as the day goes on.

What thoughts steal your hope?

When the unknowns start closing in on us, we can choose to have a continuous conversation with God saying, "God, I choose to trust You with _____. Please give me joy, hope, and peace. In Jesus name"

We don't have to rely on ourselves to get through this, we can continually ask God to help us come out of this better, stronger, and thriving in every area of our lives.

I am grateful for:

1.
2.
3.
4.
5.

"Apart from Me (Jesus) you can do nothing...Now remain in my love."
(John 15:5, 9 NIV)

It's impossible to live a Christian life without inviting Jesus in. Our own efforts just don't sustain us. We need Him. He wanted us to live wrapped in His love. He has this amazing continual flow from His heart to ours. We get to choose to let His love define us. Living in the love of God through the heart of Jesus fills a canyon in our hearts and souls that nothing else fills.

Success, friendships, relationships, work, awards...nothing quenches our hearts like the love of God. I think this is why this verse states, *"Apart from Me you can do nothing,"* because without Him there is an emptiness that accompanies every aspect of life.

In contrast, living aware of and accepting the love of God through the heart of Jesus makes life full. His love heals brokenness. His love forgives our wrong choices. His love inspires us to keep going. His love creates a feeling of acceptance that can't be found in anything else.

Do I base what I think of myself in the love of God?

God, I invite Your love to fill my heart. I invite You to do life with me moment by moment. In all the unknowns surrounding me may there be a continual flow from Your heart to mine and may I find my worth in You. In Jesus name

Great moments:

1.
2.
3.
4.
5.

In the Word, David, a man after God's heart, was an amazing warrior and king. He wrote this, *"My heart is in anguish within me, the terrors of death assail me." (Psalms 55:4 NIV)*

For him to say this his life must have been scary, and the future unknown. He goes on to talk to God about how bad everything is. The great mystery of realness in prayer and telling God about our fears, unknowns, sadness, and disappointments is that it helps. Something in our soul feels better when we tell God about everything in our heart. So after David tells God his "real," he makes a choice, *"But as for me, I trust in You (God)."*

We can follow David's example:

1. Tell God about everything in our hearts.
2. Ask Him to help in our current situation.
3. Say out loud, "I trust You, God. In Jesus name"

Choosing to trust God has nothing to do with feelings, it's a choice and a simple prayer that does something in us and around us that is beyond comprehension.

God, I trust You with me and I invite You into every area of my life. In Jesus name

I am thankful for:

1.
2.
3.
4.
5.

"So watch your step. Use your head. Make the most of every chance you get. These are desperate times!" (Ephesians 5:16 MSG)

I read this verse every morning. It pushes me forward. We can ask ourselves, "How can I make the most of every chance I have? In each conversation? In the way I do life at home? In the way I encourage others? In the way I treat those around me? In the way I grow and learn from mistakes? In the way I take risks?"

We can all ask ourselves these questions, no matter what stage of life that we are in, how old we are, what work we do, or what our hopes and dreams are.

How can I make the most out of this time mentally, emotionally, spiritually, physically to improve myself? (Writing down ways to do this in each area is motivating.)

Regardless of how hard a season is, we can, *"Make the most of every chance we get."* Knowing this is inspiring, motivating, and keeps us going.

God, instead of being overwhelmed or feeling stuck, help me to be motivated and make the most of my time, show me what steps I can take to do this. In Jesus name

I am thankful for:

1.
2.
3.
4.
5.

"Obsession with self in these matters is a dead end; attention to God leads us out into the open into a spacious, free life." *(Romans 8:6-7 MSG)*

Attention to God is about:
1. Thanking Him.
2. Giving Him our stuff (stress, worries, hopes, dreams).
3. Inviting Him to do life with us (in every area).
4. Loving Him by loving others.

Don't we all want to live a *"spacious, free life?"* That sounds amazing! Letting go of our stuff and living our life connecting with God leads us there.

What do I need to let go of?

God, Thank you for _____. I give You _____
(the things I think about, my hopes, and dreams). I invite You
into _____ (my friendships, my future, and my day).
Please help _____ (my friends or family) and show me
how to reach out to them today. In Jesus name

Great things in my life:

1.
2.
3.
4.
5.

"If we go through the hard times with him, then we're certainly going to go through the good times with him!" (Romans 8:15 MSG)

We need God to walk beside us in our hard times. Life is full of unexpected situations that can be disappointing. When we invite God into our hardship, He helps us get through it and we grow stronger.

What hard time am I going through?

In what ways can I invite God into this?

God, I invite You to walk through life with me, I want the adventure You have for me. Give me hope during this season. In Jesus name

Good things in my life:

1.
2.
3.
4.
5.

"Jesus declared, 'I am the Bread of Life.'" (John 6:35 NIV)

Jesus related Himself to things we understand. He knew that we would understand this concept of food. We eat several times a day. We need it to survive. If we don't eat then we feel hungry, unsatisfied, and it's hard to focus. The message of Jesus is simple, yet so fulfilling we can spend a lifetime letting it nourish us. This truth amazes me!

We need the love of Jesus to fill the hunger in our souls. His love and heart is the spiritual food of life. Without it we walk around hungry. Our inner hunger can lead us to try to fill this void with many other things, yet nothing except His love satisfies the crater in each soul.

Focusing on a verse, spending time in community with other believers, and talking to God fills us. We can let His heart be the echo in our mind. *"First we were loved, now we love. He loved us first." (1 John 4:19 MSG)*

Is there anything that keeps me from realizing that God's love fills my heart?

If we daily think, "I am loved by the Creator of the Universe and I am His child." This truth fills our mind, soul, and heart.

What do I think about myself?

Is it wrapped in what God says about me?

God, show me what it means to let Jesus be the *"Bread"* of my life. May Your love fill all the hunger in my soul. In Jesus name

DAY 88

What do I think about:

1.
2.
3.
4.
5.

"Yet behind everything we do is a thought, and each individual thought contributes to our overall character. How well our mind works dictates how much joy we experience, how successful we feel, and how well we interact with other people. By the grace of God, each moment is a new beginning, a new dawn for potential." (Tommy Newberry, The Secret to a Joy Filled Life)

"It's in Him we find out who we are and what we are living for!" (Ephesians 1:11 MSG)

Moments. Each one of them is precious and "a new beginning." A moment cannot be re-lived. A word cannot be unspoken. An experience cannot be perfectly recreated. Knowing this truth about moments can drive us to live each one to the fullest.

Living life to the fullest requires living grounded in the truth that we are known and loved by God, continually thinking about the good in life, and giving to others.

How am I going to live my moments today?

God, I give You my moments. I invite You to help me to think about the good in life, which will lead me to give to others. May my life be built on what You think about me. In Jesus name

DAY 89

What am I grateful for?

1.
2.
3.
4.
5.

"Leaving the crowd behind, they took him along, just as he was, in the boat. There were also other boats with him. A furious squall came up, and the waves broke over the boat, so that it was nearly swamped. Jesus was in the stern, sleeping on a cushion. The disciples woke him and said to him, 'Teacher, don't you care if we drown?' He got up, rebuked the wind and said to the waves, 'Quiet! Be still!' Then the wind died down and it was completely calm. He said to his disciples, 'Why are you so afraid? Do you still have no faith?'" (Mark 4:36-41 NIV)

When summer is almost over, I always hang on to that last moment of the season. To have one last summer escapade I took my five kids tubing. My 9,12,14, and 16-year old kids really wanted to go, and I was thrilled when my 18-year-old son agreed to go also. Arriving in Dahlonega, there were no other cars in the parking lot and I noticed a few clouds in the sky, but I didn't think this would stop our adventure.

Getting into our tubes and floating along was so peaceful. All my kids together, enjoying a great moment! A little way down the river gentle raindrops started to land on our shoulders and faces, and then it started pouring, but it was all part of the experience. In the distance thunder came rolling in and lightning streaked across the sky. We were almost finished with the river course, but when that bolt of lightning hit, it was clear we needed to head to the path, which would lead us on a hike back to the entrance. At this point, we are in a torrential downpour!

All of us, with our many temperaments and personality traits, responded differently. Addi, my sixteen-year-old daughter, was thinking logically. Owin, my eighteen-year-old, was cracking jokes. "Mom, God starts biting His nails when you take us on an adventure..." "People are missing their guardian angel because He has to give you so many..." My sweet, calm, enneagram 9, Eben, (age 14) was encouraging me, telling me that I am a great mom and this wasn't a dumb idea. John E, my generally talkative 12-year-old, was strangely quiet and aloof. The youngest, Anden, (age 9) was surprisingly brave and ready to lead us all to the car. I was laughing, I do that at awkward moments, for I led my kids into a storm, ignored all of the warning signs, and jumped into another adventure.

For a mile we quickly walked along a trail that looked like a river itself as thunder echoed and lightning cracked around us. I kept thinking, "We are walking in one huge puddle in a lightning storm...Not my wisest choice." We continued to walk, knowing we would have to get back in the water to cross the river to get to our car at some point. However, at the last minute Owin saw an old bridge and, as I held my breath, we crossed it safely.

We all responded to the same storm differently...I wonder how all of the disciples responded to their storm? I wonder how all the other people in boats nearby reacted as their solid ground rocked in the mighty waves.

To reflect, we can ask ourselves, "How do I respond to storms?" Some of us are terrified, some of us pray, some of us ignore the situation while others barrel through it, some of us encourage others, some of us laugh to keep from crying. Life can feel like a rocking boat sometimes. Being a teenager is hard enough without a pandemic. Some seasons can feel like a storm after storm.

Jesus spoke to the wind and the waves. He stopped the storm and brought calm. Knowing and embracing this creates a peace in us that nothing external can touch. Jesus can calm the storm in our mind and in our heart and create calm, because He loves us with a love that is bigger than any storm.

You are almost finished with this book, I want to encourage you to think back and ask yourself a few questions:

How have I responded to the storms in my life?

Am I in a storm? Or do I see a storm on the horizon?

How am I responding today?

Will I invite Jesus into it?

Jesus, I invite You into my storm. Help me to choose to trust You while You are calming this storm. I accept Your great love as my identity. In Jesus name

DAY 90

What makes me smile?

1.
2.
3.
4.
5.

"I've found the recipe for being happy whether full or hungry, hands full or hands empty. Whatever I have, wherever I am, I can make it through anything in the One who makes me who I am." (Philippians 4:12-13 MSG)

Life isn't easy. We go through ups and downs emotionally, in relationships, at school, at work, and in our dreams and goals.

What feels hard in my life?

How am I dealing with this?

Is this a healthy way to deal with this?

"I can make it through ANYTHING in the ONE who makes me who I am." I love this translation. God is the one who makes us who we are. We can find our worth in Him. His heart is love, so to Him we are all lovable. This truth gives me great peace when it feels like life is tough.

In my thoughts, do I constantly remember that I am lovable and have great worth simply because He made me and He loves me?

God, remind me often who I am in You. In Jesus name

KEEP GOING!

"...I (Jesus) have come that they may have life to the full!" *(John 10:10)*

Jesus has a full life for everyone, it may not mean a perfect life, but our heart can be full because we are growing in our relationship with God who loves us and is FOR us.

Spending time with God is simple:

Start off thankful and jumpstart your brain by asking yourself, what are five good things in my life? What am I thankful for?

Read a Bible verse and ask yourself questions about how this verse applies to you personally.

Invite Jesus into every aspect of life (thoughts, relationships, moments, dreams, school/work, struggles).

Repeatedly doing these three things changes our perspective. When we *think* thankful, we *feel* thankful and we live this out by the way we treat others. Doing this affects everything in our life. When we grow in our faith, our life becomes better!

NOTE FROM THE AUTHOR...

Friends,

YOU MADE IT THROUGH 90 DAYS! You also created a habit that you can continue always. Choose Life to the Fullest (books 1, 2, and 3) were written for teens who I have mentored or counseled, and my own sixteen-year-old son, who was consumed with negative thoughts. God made us all a "masterpiece," yet the negative voices can be so loud that we forget to listen to God.

By daily starting our day with God and inviting Jesus in, something mysterious changes in us. After doing this format of daily devotions, my son randomly said, "Mom, I think I like myself." His time with Jesus and thinking thankful changed his perspective.

Every morning, I wake up and write 5 thankful, read a verse and ask myself questions, and invite Jesus in. WHY? Because, this habit creates life to the FULL! I hope and pray for that for each of you. It is my prayer that you know that you are loved and treasured by the heart of God, and He is always pursuing a relationship with you. Jesus wants you to invite Him into everything.

Blessings!
Becca

REFERENCES

Eldredge, J. (2020). *Get your life back: Everyday practices for a world gone mad.* Thomas Nelson.

Foster, R., J. (1992). *Prayer: Finding the heart's true home.* Harper Collins.

Leaf, C. (2007). *Switch on your brain: The key to peak happiness, thinking and health.* Baker Books.

Manning, B. (2014). *Abba's child: The cry of the heart for intimate belonging.* Tyndale House Publishers

Newberry, T. (2012). *40 days to a joy-filled life.* Tyndale House Publishers.

Printed in the United States
By Bookmasters